THE HODDER WAYLAND ATLAS OF
RAIN FORESTS

Anna Lewington

HODDER
Wayland

an imprint of Hodder Children's Books

In association with World Wide Fund For Nature and Forests For Life campaign

HODDER WAYLAND ATLAS OF
RAIN FORESTS

Produced for Wayland Publishers Ltd by
Roger Coote Publishing
Gissing's Farm, Fressingfield, Eye
Suffolk IP21 5SH, England

First published in Great Britain in 1996
by Wayland (Publishers) Ltd

Reprinted in 2000 by Hodder Wayland,
an imprint of Hodder Children's Books

Designed by Tim Mayer
Map artwork by Peter Bull

© Hodder Wayland 1996

British Library Cataloguing in Publication Data
Wayland Atlas of Rain Forests. – (Wayland Thematic Atlases)
1.Rain forests – maps – Juvenile literature
2.Rain forest ecology – Juvenile literature
I. Atlas of Rain Forests
574.5'2642'0223

ISBN 0 7502 2520 3

Printed and bound in Italy by G. Canale & C.S.p.A., Turin

ACKNOWLEDGEMENTS

The author would like to thank the many people who helped with the provision of information for this Atlas, in particular: Claire Billington, for her assistance with the rain forest maps and background information, and also Neil Cox, Harriet Gillett and Bill Oates, all of the World Conservation Monitoring Centre.

Special thanks are also due to: Keith Brown, Mark Pilgrim and Nick Ellerton, Chester Zoo; Martin Cheek, Royal Botanic Gardens, Kew; Marcus Colchester, World Rain Forest Movement; Alan Hamilton, World Wide Fund for Nature; Laura Hastings, Royal Botanic Gardens, Kew; Tony Juniper, Friends of the Earth; Barbara Lowry, Royal Botanic Gardens, Kew; Jo Mee, World Wide Fund for Nature; Douglas Richardson, London Zoo; Valerie Shawyer, The Hawk and Owl Trust; Piers Vitebsky, The Scott Polar Research Institute; Alan Watson Featherstone, Trees for Life; Tom Foose, IUCN/SSC Asian Rhino Specialist Group; and to Edward Parker for his comments on the text.

The kind assistance of the following people is also gratefully acknowledged: Staff of the Alaskan Federation of Natives; Bryan Alexander; Heidi Cameron; Ros Coles; Nigel Dudley; Nina Epton; Jane Fitzpatrick; Sheila and Andrew Gray; Pat Griggs; Jonathan King; Nicholas Martland; Jonathon Mazower; Peter Ramshaw; Doug Shiel; Peter Vinsen; David Wege; and Angie Zelter.

CONTENTS

World map

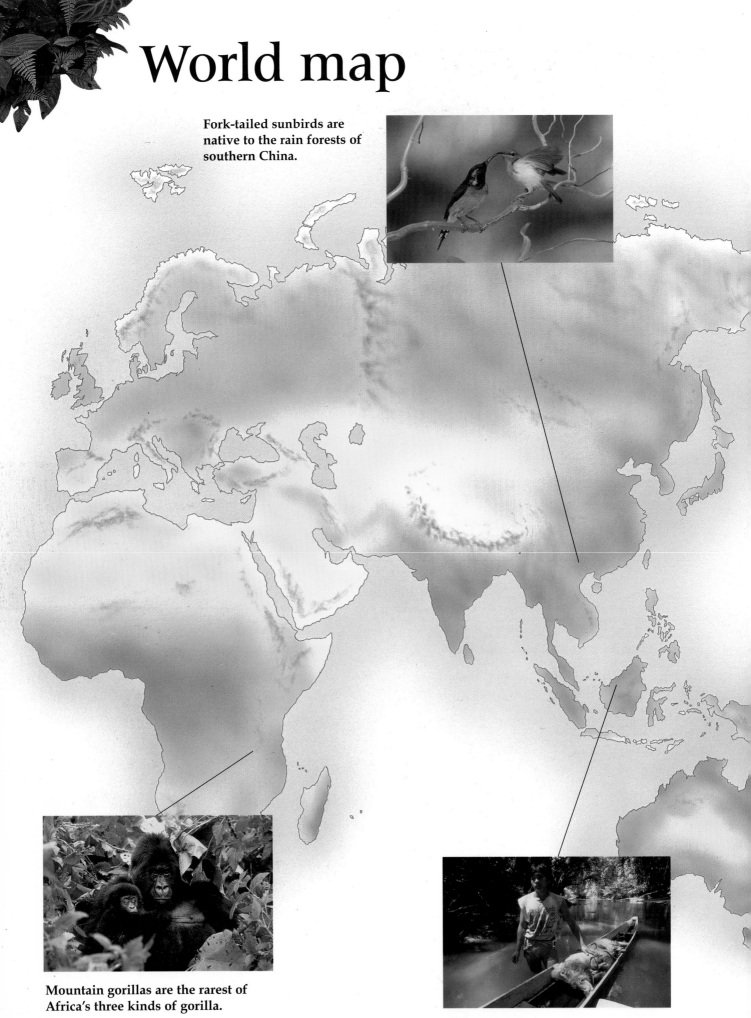

Fork-tailed sunbirds are native to the rain forests of southern China.

Mountain gorillas are the rarest of Africa's three kinds of gorilla.

The Penan are one of many tribal peoples who live in the rain forests of Borneo in Southeast Asia.

The endangered northern spotted owl has helped draw attention to the destruction of North America's ancient temperate forests on which it depends.

The biggest bird-eating spider in the world lives in northern South America.

Tourists gathered at the base of *Tane Mahuta*, a huge kauri pine in New Zealand's North island.

How to Use this Atlas

REGIONAL PAGE

On the pages with the continent maps you will find a globe. This shows you where in the world the continent is situated.

The text on these pages introduces you to the various types of rain forest environment there, the forms of life they contain and how they are changing.

The *Wayland Atlas of Rain Forests* contains information about different types of rain forest around the world. You can find out in detail about many rain-forest peoples, animals, trees and other plants.

There are two different kinds of map and two sorts of text in this book.

MAINLAND ASIA

In mainland Asia rain forests and seasonal monsoon forests are found from India in the west to Vietnam in the east. However, in recent decades large areas of forest have been cut down to make way for rice paddies and plantations of cash crops or logged for valuable timber. This has left the forests greatly fragmented and many of their animals and plants have become very rare. In India's Western Ghats, for example, the wild dog, sloth bear, tiger, mugger crocodile and the gaur (a rare cattle species), are all endangered due to habitat loss.

In Bangladesh less than 5 per cent of the country's rain and monsoon forest survives. The largest area is a vast coastal mangrove forest, the Sundurbans, where tigers can still be found. Further east, Thailand has only 15 per cent of its original rain forest – largely due to logging – and Myanmar has now become a major source of teak and other tropical hardwoods. In Cambodia and Vietnam large areas of forest were destroyed by bombing during the Vietnam War (1954–75) but the region still contains Asian elephants, Javan rhinos and the kouprey, another rare cattle species.

To the north, patches of rain forest extend into southern China. Here, and further west along this northern boundary, the rain forests gradually change into subtropical and then temperate rain forests but the limits of each have not been clearly defined.

People have been living in Asia for about one million years and many types of domesticated animals and plants originated there. The forests are still home to a large number of indigenous peoples, but their unique ways of life are increasingly threatened by modern development.

Tigers are now very rare in India, and a number of reserves have been set up to try to help protect them.

FEATURE PAGE

The text on the feature pages tells you about particular species of trees, plants, animals or indigenous peoples living in the rain forests.

You can find out about at least one of the special plants, animals and people from each region using these pages.

The Nayaka

About 1,400 Nayaka people live in the south-western foothills of the Nilgiris – a hilly plateau also known as the Blue Mountains – in the southern Indian state of Tamil Nadu and the adjoining parts of Kerala. This diverse region has many different types of forest, including lowland evergreen, montane *shola* forest and bamboo forest.

The Nayaka live in an area known as the Wynaad, in small communities made up of between one and five huts. The huts are built in forest clearings. They are sometimes made from strips of flattened bamboo and have roofs thatched with grass. The Nayaka move to a new part of the forest and build new huts every 6 to 18 months. They gather much of the food they need from the forest, including birds' eggs, wild yams and honey – a favourite food. The Nayaka also fish and hunt animals, and gather firewood and building materials from the forest. They sometimes spend one or more days on gathering expeditions, always carrying a woven basket, a curved knife for cutting vegetation and digging stick with them. Sometimes they spend the night in a cave.

The Nayaka trade forest produce with other people in the region, and wear shop-bought clothes. Some work on the large rubber, tea and coffee plantations that have been set up in their area, but they believe that they must try and live in the way that their ancestors did.

One group of Nayaka, called the Sholanayaka, make their homes in caves and live mainly by hunting, gathering and fishing. Once a year a special celebration is held and offerings are made to the spirits who control their lives.

HEALERS AND MAGICIANS

The Nayaka are regarded by others in the Nilgiris as having special supernatural powers and medicinal skills. Because of this they are generally feared, but are sought after for special cures and ritual objects they can find in the forest. Nayaka shamans are also believed to be able to bring prosperity and success.

The Sholanayaka are one of several different tribal peoples who live in the Nilgiri region.

60

REGIONAL PAGE

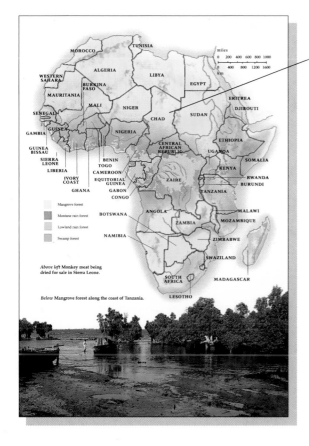

The big regional maps show the different types of rain forest that can be found in a particular region or continent.

The types of forest shown on these maps include tropical lowland rain forest, tropical montane rain forest, temperate rain forest, mangrove forest and swamp. Next to the map is a key to help you identify them.

FEATURE PAGE

The maps on the feature pages show you where a particular people, animal or tree lives, as well as the main towns, rivers, hills and valleys. In the corner of most of these maps you will find a small map of the continent, which shows you where the area of the bigger map is located.

The World's Rain Forests

The name 'rain forest' was first used at the end of the nineteenth century to describe forests that grow in constantly wet conditions. Today, scientists define rain forests as forests that receive more than 2,000 mm of rain (moisture) evenly spread throughout the year. Although the best known rain forests are found in tropical regions – between the Tropics of Cancer and Capricorn – rain forests also occur in temperate areas of the world.

TROPICAL RAIN FORESTS

Tropical rain forests are found in a belt around the Equator, where temperatures and rainfall are very high all year round. There is very little variation between the seasons and the trees are mostly evergreen.

Further away from the Equator, to the north and south of the rain forest belt, where temperatures and rainfall are lower, the seasons are more distinct. Here, rain forests become tropical seasonal forests. In Asia they are known as 'monsoon forests', as their leaves appear at the beginning of the annual monsoon. Although they are not as extensive or as rich in plant and animal species, tropical seasonal forests have much in common with equatorial rain forests and they are known together as 'moist forests'.

Tropical rain forests are divided into two main types, according to their height above sea level. These are lowland and montane rain forests. Lowland rain forests are the most widespread, but have also suffered the most destruction. These contain the richest communities of plants in the world. Montane rain forests generally occur from about 900 m upwards on hills or mountains in the tropics. Here, the hot, sticky humidity of the lowland rain forests gives way to a cooler, damper climate. Mists often surround the upper layers of the forest, giving rise to the name 'cloud forest'.

Millions of tribal people have lived in tropical rain forests for thousands of years without destroying them.

Botanists recognize as many as 40 different types of lowland tropical rain forest, which differ because of rainfall, soils and drainage patterns. These include semi-evergreen, heath and bamboo forests. Mangrove is a special kind of evergreen rain forest that grows in salty coastal waters which are rich in silt. Another kind of flooded forest is found along the banks of rain forest rivers. These areas, which include the *várzea* and *igapo* forests of the Amazon, are often swamped or flooded either permanently or at different times during the year with fresh water.

Tropical rain forests are famous for their vast array of plant and animal life, representing over 50 per cent of all species on earth, but they are also home to millions of indigenous people. Having lived in the forests for thousands of years, they have enriched many areas by planting useful trees. They know how to use the forests' natural resources in ways that do not endanger the survival of the rain forests and their plants and animals.

Tropical rain forests around the world are still being felled at an alarming rate: about 142,000 square kilometres per year. The main causes of destruction include logging, mining, the building of new roads, and industrial and agricultural development projects.

Right This boy is a member of the Baka, a group of Pygmies who live in the rain forests of Cameroon, Africa.

Below The world's largest flower, *Rafflesia arnoldii*, is found only in the rain forests of Southeast Asia.

A flying squirrel which inhabits the temperate rain forests of North America.

TEMPERATE RAIN FORESTS

Temperate rain forests are thought to exist in a number of different locations throughout the world but their precise definition and the area they occupy has not been fully agreed on by scientists. However, the best known type of temperate rain forest, coastal temperate rain forest, has been defined and mapped in some detail.

Coastal temperate rain forests have three things in common: they are close to oceans, found in mountainous regions and, like tropical rain forests, have high annual rainfall (over 2,000 mm). These forests are very complex in structure, and are influenced by the effects of ocean currents and sea winds. They contain some of the oldest and largest trees in the world. These tower above a mosaic of smaller trees and shrubs and fallen logs, covered with mosses, ferns and fungi.

Because of continued logging activity, coastal temperate rain forest is now very rare, making up only 0.8 per cent of all forests on earth. However, it once covered over twice as much land – some 30–40 million ha. Iceland, the west coasts of Ireland and Scotland, a narrow crescent along the Black Sea in Turkey, and Soviet Georgia all once contained coastal temperate rain forest. Japan and Norway are said to still have some, but its precise extent has not been mapped.

The largest continuous area of coastal temperate rain forest in the world is in North America, stretching from the Alaskan Peninsula southwards to Oregon's Siuslaw River. The largest area still undisturbed by loggers is in British Columbia, Canada. However, there, as elsewhere, the global demand for wood products continues to threaten these ancient forests and concerted action is being demanded by conservationists to save the little that remains.

Above A park ranger in Chile stands guard beside one of the largest, oldest alerce trees in the world.

Below Part of one of the carved wooden totem poles of the Tlingit people.

NORTH AMERICA

North America stretches from Canada and the USA in the north, through Mexico and Central America, as far south as Panama. It also includes the islands of the Caribbean Sea. In this huge area, with its broad range of climates, there are two main types of rain forest: temperate and tropical.

TEMPERATE RAIN FORESTS

North America contains the largest continuous area of coastal temperate rain forest in the world: 40–50 per cent of the world total. It extends from the state of Oregon in the south to Alaska's Aleutian mountain range in the north.

Coastal temperate rain forests are among the most complex natural environments on earth and the number of different forms of life they contain makes them comparable to tropical rain forests. Buffeted by coastal winds and rain storms, the forests receive high levels of moisture all year round. Fallen trunks and branches carpet much of the forest floor and these are covered with mosses, ferns and fungi. As the fallen logs decay, they provide the nutrients needed for young tree seedlings to become established. Above the ground, the constant moisture in the air and the mild climate create the perfect conditions for mosses to grow on tree branches, often hanging down in graceful curtains.

North American coastal rain forests contain about twenty five tree species and are dominated by conifer trees: chiefly cedar, hemlock and spruce. Among these are some of the oldest and largest trees in the world.

Right Pileated woodpeckers at their nest hole feeding young.

The dense area of uncut forest on the left of this picture contrasts sharply with the area on the right, in which almost all of the trees have been cut down to supply the huge demand for timber.

ALASKA
(USA)

PACIFIC
OCEAN

R O C K Y

CANADA

M O U N T A I N S

USA

ATLANTIC
OCEAN

0   500   1000   km
0   200   400   600   miles

Temperate rain forest

MEXICO   GULF OF
MEXICO

About 350 species of birds and animals live in the forests along with hundreds of fungi and lichen species and thousands of insects, mites, spiders and organisms in the soil.

There has been widespread logging in the rain forests: so far over 90 per cent has been felled.

Despite the creation of parks and reserves, many animals and birds are now endangered because it is difficult for them to survive in the small patches of forest that remain.

Animals and birds affected include bear, deer, elk and salamander species, the spotted owl, pileated woodpecker and marbled murrelet.

TROPICAL RAIN FORESTS

Although they now cover a relatively small area, the rain forests of Central America and Southern Mexico are among the richest habitats on earth, in terms of the number of plant and animal species they contain. Both Central America and the Caribbean are especially rich in birdlife. The tiny country of El Salvador has 350 bird species, while Panama has 700 – more than the whole of North America's temperate rain forests. The region is visited by at least 225 species of migratory birds from North and South America, and many North American species overwinter there.

Two young Embera Indian children from Darién in Panama.

The northernmost limit of the tropical rain forests of the Americas is in southern Mexico. In this country, rain forests are now found in three separate blocks, covering about 150,000 square kilometres. Although this is less than half the area that existed 35 years ago, the forests are still home to a great variety of plants and animals including green iguanas, quetzals, spider monkeys and jaguars.

Many plant species are also native to the region. Jamaica has 900 species of plant that are found nowhere else, as well as 20 amphibian, 26 bird and 27 reptile species. A number of important tropical crops are native to Central America and the Caribbean, including vanilla (also found in South America), allspice and papayas.

Central America has a large number of indigenous peoples whose lifestyles reflect a deep understanding of the rain forest. The most numerous of these are the Mayan peoples of southern Mexico, Guatemala, Belize and Honduras, who now number more than 8 million.

COLUMBUS AND THE RAIN FOREST

'Its lands are high… and filled with trees of a thousand kinds and tall, so that they seem to touch the sky. I am told that they never lose their foliage, and this I can believe, for I saw them as green and lovely as they are in Spain in May, and some of them were flowering, some bearing fruit, and some at another stage according to their nature.'

Christopher Columbus's description of the forests of Hispaniola (Haiti and Dominican Republic) – the first written account of a rain forest.

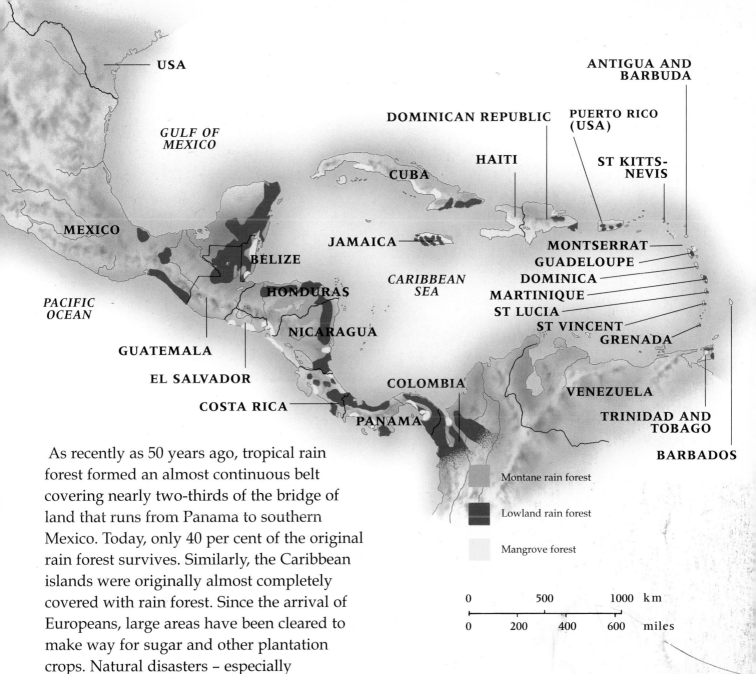

USA

GULF OF
MEXICO

ANTIGUA AND
BARBUDA

DOMINICAN REPUBLIC

PUERTO RICO
(USA)

HAITI

ST KITTS-
NEVIS

CUBA

MEXICO

JAMAICA

BELIZE

CARIBBEAN
SEA

MONTSERRAT
GUADELOUPE
DOMINICA
MARTINIQUE
ST LUCIA
ST VINCENT
GRENADA

HONDURAS

PACIFIC
OCEAN

NICARAGUA

GUATEMALA

EL SALVADOR

COLOMBIA

VENEZUELA

COSTA RICA

PANAMA

TRINIDAD AND
TOBAGO

BARBADOS

Montane rain forest

Lowland rain forest

Mangrove forest

0		500		1000	km
0	200	400		600	miles

As recently as 50 years ago, tropical rain forest formed an almost continuous belt covering nearly two-thirds of the bridge of land that runs from Panama to southern Mexico. Today, only 40 per cent of the original rain forest survives. Similarly, the Caribbean islands were originally almost completely covered with rain forest. Since the arrival of Europeans, large areas have been cleared to make way for sugar and other plantation crops. Natural disasters – especially hurricanes – have also destroyed areas made vulnerable by large-scale deforestation.

Bromeliads growing in a tropical rain forest on the island of Tobago in the Caribbean.

15

The Tlingit

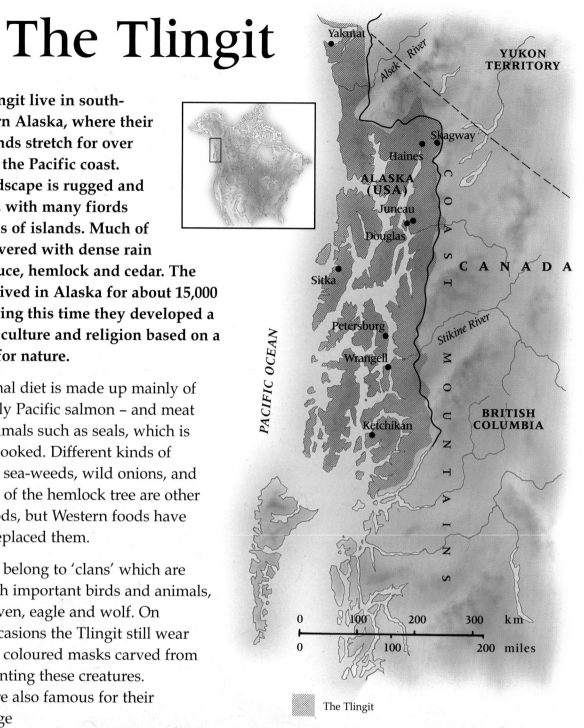

The Tlingit live in south-western Alaska, where their traditional lands stretch for over 800 km along the Pacific coast. Here, the landscape is rugged and mountainous, with many fiords and thousands of islands. Much of the land is covered with dense rain forests of spruce, hemlock and cedar. The Tlingit have lived in Alaska for about 15,000 years and during this time they developed a sophisticated culture and religion based on a deep respect for nature.

Their traditional diet is made up mainly of fish – especially Pacific salmon – and meat from sea mammals such as seals, which is eaten raw or cooked. Different kinds of berries, edible sea-weeds, wild onions, and the inner bark of the hemlock tree are other traditional foods, but Western foods have now largely replaced them.

Tlingit people belong to 'clans' which are associated with important birds and animals, such as the raven, eagle and wolf. On ceremonial occasions the Tlingit still wear large, brightly coloured masks carved from wood, representing these creatures. The people are also famous for their traditional large wooden houses, their wooden battle helmets and their woven five-cornered *chilkat* blankets, also worn for special ceremonies.

This Tlingit woman is holding a pole on which salmon have been dried and smoked.

The Tlingit

16

Europeans first made contact with the Tlingit about 250 years ago. Since then, much of their culture has had to change. Today, the Tlingit are trying to strengthen their traditions, and their own language is now taught in schools. In recent years the US government has encouraged the Tlingit to develop fishing and timber businesses on their own land. However, many fear that these economic activities will destroy more of their culture and their forests in the future.

Above A traditional Tlingit canoe. Craft like this were originally used for catching salmon.

Above The designs on these Tlingit costumes – including a *chilkat* blanket (centre) and appliqué and button blankets – represent the different clans to which the people belong.

SALMON PEOPLE

The Tlingit believe that the natural world is full of spirits. They believe that the salmon they catch are really people, who live in large houses deep down in the sea. The salmon allow themselves to be caught and eaten, but when the Tlingit return their bones to the rivers, they turn into people again.

The Western Red Cedar

The western red cedar is native to the ancient forests of western North America. Like the Douglas fir (which can grow up to 90 m) and western hemlock, western red cedar is a true forest giant. It can grow up to 70 m in height and measure 5 m around its trunk. Maturing slowly, it can live for up to 1,000 years.

Although the tree is cone-shaped when young, the top of the tree broadens with age. Enormous branches can develop which grow downwards at first but then curve upwards, forming one or more rings around the trunk. Mature trees have a thick, soft bark which is dark purplish to red-brown in colour. This has wide ridges and breaks into strips and 'plates' as the tree grows. The base of the trunk also becomes fluted as it matures. The trees' evergreen leaves have a very fragrant smell, like apples or pineapples, often scenting the air around them.

The western red cedar is one of the most important of the coastal temperate rain forest trees and plays a major part in maintaining the complex forest ecosystem. Bearing the brunt of coastal winds and rain storms, it protects the shallow-rooted, faster-growing trees that grow beneath it among the litter of logs and fallen branches. These less-hardy, deciduous trees include birch, maple, alder, aspen and willow species. Beneath them, shrubs, ferns, fungi, lichens and mosses abound. Together they create a large number of habitats for wildlife.

Above **Western red cedar foliage and cones.**

The massive trunk and one of the downward-curving branches of a mature western red cedar tree.

THE MANY USES OF RED CEDAR

The western red cedar has always been very important to the lives of the Native American peoples of the Pacific Northwest. Respected and revered for its great size and age, the tree's strong, rot-resistant timber was formerly used for a great many purposes including boards and planking for houses, dishes, arrow shafts, masks, rattles, drums, fishing floats and paddles. Huge trunks were hollowed out to make ocean-going canoes, and carved to make elaborate totem poles.

Colourful faces painted on to a carved Alaskan totem pole, made from cedar wood.

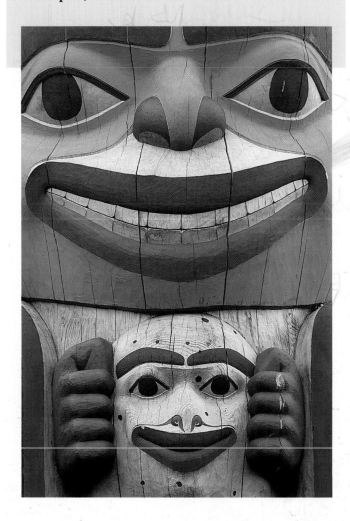

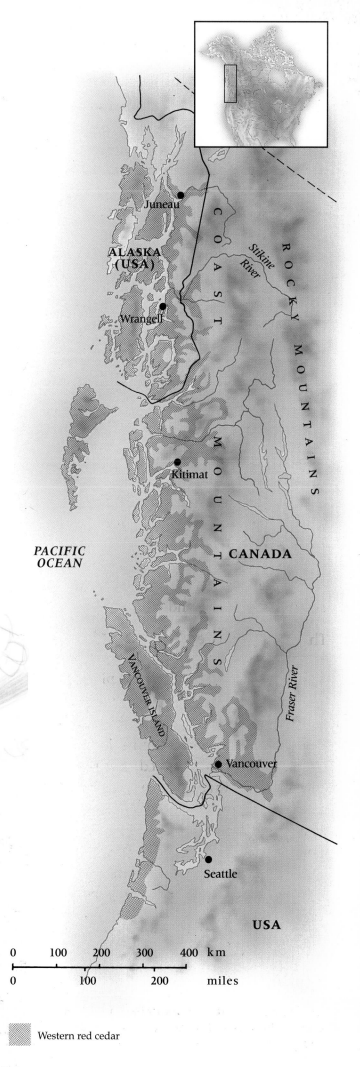

0   100   200   300   400   k m

0   100   200   miles

Western red cedar

19

The Spotted Owl

The spotted owl is found in a broad band of western North America, from southern British Columbia in the north to central Mexico in the south. Because the owls are so widely spread, experts recognize three different populations.

The birds living furthest north – from northern California to British Columbia – are usually referred to as northern spotted owls. They are a dark, rich red-brown on their back and head, mottled with light brown, and have white spots on the head and the back of the neck. They are of medium-size, measuring from 405–480 mm, with rounded heads and large eyes.

Northern spotted owls live only in the dense, ancient forests that run along the north-west Pacific coast. They need large areas of this 'old-growth' forest for feeding and nesting and have been unable to settle where the forests have been disturbed by logging or replaced by plantations. They nest in holes in the trunks of large, ancient trees.

CANADA

Seattle

WASHINGTON

CASCADE RANGE

PACIFIC OCEAN

Portland

U S A

OREGON

COAST RANGES

SIERRA NEVADA

NEVADA

Sacramento

San Francisco

CALIFORNIA

Northern spotted owls

km 0 100 200 300

miles 0 100 200

Right A northern spotted owl perches in a moss-covered Douglas fir tree in south-western Oregon, USA.

SAVING THE OWLS; SAVING THE FOREST

In 1990 the northern spotted owl was classified as a threatened species and it became illegal to do anything that might endanger it further. A serious argument began between the loggers – who planned to cut down much of the remaining old-growth forests that are the owls' home – and conservationists. About 90 per cent of the ancient forests of the Pacific North-west have already been felled and only about 3,000 pairs of spotted owls remain.

A northern spotted owl swoops down out of the darkeness to catch a woodrat on the forest floor.

The owls are only active at night and eat mostly woodrats and flying squirrels. They hunt by perching quietly on a branch and then seizing any suitable prey with their powerful feet.

Spotted owls can be difficult to see at night, but if found roosting during the daytime, or on their nests, they will let people watch them from only a few centimetres away.

Northern flying squirrels are one of the spotted owl's main foods.

The Kuna

The Kuna are one of the three indigenous peoples of Panama. Today, about 30,000 Kuna live in 60 villages on some of the tiny, coral islands off the Caribbean coast – the San Blas islands. Each day they fish, and cross the sea in dug-out canoes to work in their gardens on the coast where they grow a large number of crops.

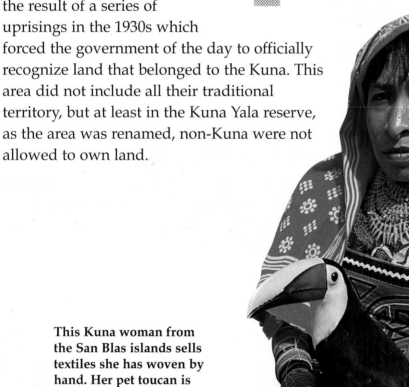

Unlike many indigenous groups, the Kuna own the land they now live on. This is the result of a series of uprisings in the 1930s which forced the government of the day to officially recognize land that belonged to the Kuna. This area did not include all their traditional territory, but at least in the Kuna Yala reserve, as the area was renamed, non-Kuna were not allowed to own land.

The Kuna Yala Reserve

This Kuna woman from the San Blas islands sells textiles she has woven by hand. Her pet toucan is perched on her lap.

In the 1970s a new road was begun at the western end of the Kuna Yala reserve and the Kuna knew that this would allow squatters to flood in and take over their lands. With their long history of fighting to defend their rights, the Kuna decided to take action to save their forests and their culture. They set up the Kuna Wildlands Project and became the world's first indigenous people to establish an internationally recognized forest reserve.

Below **The traditional designs of these colourful molas are similar to those used by the ancient Mayas.**

Above **The thatched house of a Kuna family on one of the San Blas islands.**

The project divides the reserve into four types of protected area, including an area for agriculture and a cultural area, and a core area in which only scientific research and tourism are allowed. Scientists or tourists must pay to visit the reserve.

MOLAS

Kuna women are famous for their beautiful traditional dress and especially for their brightly coloured molas. These are pieces of appliquéd fabric with stylized designs that are worn as blouse fronts. Each mola is hand-sewn and takes about two months to make. It is coloured with mostly natural dyes.

The Resplendant Quetzal

The resplendant quetzal is one of the world's most striking and beautiful birds. With glittering emerald green feathers above and crimson plumage below, the resplendant quetzal glows from head to foot. It has a magnificent tail, made up of graceful curving plumes, two of which can grow to nearly a metre long. The male quetzal – which has brighter plumage than the female – shows off these tail feathers during spectacular swooping display flights above the trees. After each breeding season these feathers are shed and then they regrow.

Quetzals sit very still on a branch before swooping quickly down to feed and then returning to their branch.

Mérida

CARIBBEAN SEA

Villahermosa

BELIZE

Belize City

MEXICO

GUATEMALA

HONDURAS

Guatemala

Tegucigalpa

San Salvador

NICARAGUA

Managua

0 100 200 300 400 500 km

0   100   200   300   miles

EL SALVADOR

COSTA RICA

Resplendant quetzals

San José

Panama

PANAMA

PACIFIC OCEAN

24

Although they also eat insects, and when young, small frogs, lizards and snails, quetzals are specialized fruit-eaters. They are particularly fond of wild avocados and eat at least 18 different species. Quetzals depend on them so much that they disappear from an area if the avocado trees are cut down, or have simply stopped fruiting.

Avocado trees depend on the quetzals too. The fruit is swallowed whole but the hard seed is regurgitated later, allowing a new tree to grow from it. In this way, avocado trees can spread to different parts of the forest.

Quetzals nest in holes which they make in rotting tree trunks. Both male and female birds help to incubate the two sky-blue eggs that are laid, and both play a part in looking after the young.

The quetzal's natural range extends from southern Mexico to western Panama, but it breeds only in areas of cloud forest, above a height of 1,500 m. The number of quetzals has decreased greatly in recent years because of forest destruction and because it has been hunted for souvenirs. No one knows how many are left.

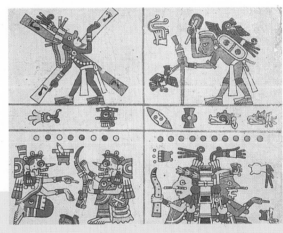

Above **A scene from an ancient Mixtec Indian manuscript showing (top right) a trader carrying prized quetzal birds.**

BIRD OF THE GODS

The resplendant quetzal was considered divine by the Aztecs of Mexico and worshipped as god of the air. Only members of the royal family were allowed to wear its tail feathers, which were taken from live birds. Anyone who killed a quetzal would be put to death. The quetzal was also sacred to other Central American Indians such as the Toltecs and Mayas.

A male quetzal feeds its young at the entrance to its nest.

Chicle – the Chewing Gum Tree

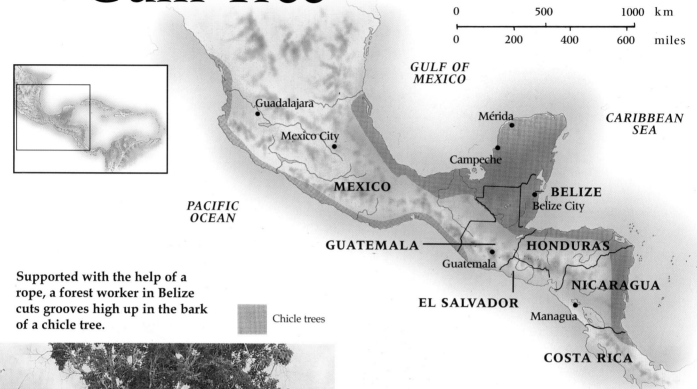

GULF OF
MEXICO

CARIBBEAN
SEA

Guadalajara

Mérida

Mexico City

Campeche

MEXICO

BELIZE
Belize City

PACIFIC
OCEAN

GUATEMALA

HONDURAS

Guatemala

NICARAGUA

EL SALVADOR

Managua

COSTA RICA

Chicle trees

Supported with the help of a rope, a forest worker in Belize cuts grooves high up in the bark of a chicle tree.

Over a thousand years ago, Mayan peoples discovered that the milky sap known as latex, produced by the chicle or sapodilla tree, thickened on heating, and produced a gum that could be chewed. Chicle trees were widely cultivated for this purpose in Central America, but grow naturally in the greatest numbers in the Yucatán peninsula (part of Mexico, Guatemala and Belize). Chewing gum was also enjoyed by the Aztecs, and the word *chicle* is derived from the Aztec word for juice or sap.

Today, *chicleros,* who are often Mayan Indians, still gather chicle latex from wild trees for the modern production of chewing gum. Some chicle trees can grow to over 75 m in height. A tree must be over 20 years old to give a good yield, and latex flows well only in the wet season – generally between July and December. The trees are tapped by cutting zig-zag grooves in the bark; the latex flows slowly down the grooves into a container at the base of the tree.

After collection, the latex is heated until it thickens and it is then moulded into blocks. Later, sweeteners and flavourings are added. Today, the base of most chewing gum is a blend of several kinds of natural latexes from rain forest trees, including chicle, as well as waxes, resins, plastics and artificial rubber.

This worker has cut grooves into the bark of a chicle tree allowing the sap to run down and be collected.

The man below is preparing a ball of natural rubber with latex tapped from wild Brazilian rubber trees.

WILD SAPS FOR INDUSTRY

A great array of rain forest trees produce gums, resins and latexes, often as part of their natural defence system against insect and animal predators. Rain forest peoples learnt long ago how to make use of many of these and their experience has led to commercial useage today in an enormous range of goods, from printing inks to pharmaceuticals, car tyres and food. The most famous latex is natural rubber derived from Amazonian trees.

The Eyelash Viper

The eyelash viper lives in the rain forests of southern Mexico, the whole of Central America (except El Salvador), and parts of Colombia, Venezuela and Ecuador. It is found from near sea level to about 1,000 m in Mexico and Guatemala, and at higher altitudes further south – up to 2,640 m in Colombia. These snakes are about 40–60 cm long and vary in colour and patterning, from a uniform brown to brilliant yellow, red, green or grey with black, red or other contrasting spots.

Eyelash vipers are adapted perfectly to life in the trees, and use their colouring to disguise themselves from their prey and hide from danger. The spectacular yellow-coloured eyelash viper, for example, uses its vivid golden colour to camouflage itself perfectly among ripe palm fruit, and catches the small animals that visit the fruit. The viper eats a range of creatures including frogs, lizards, small birds and mammals. It is nocturnal and hangs by its prehensile tail waiting for its prey.

A yellow eyelash viper on a *Heliconia* flower eating a lizard.

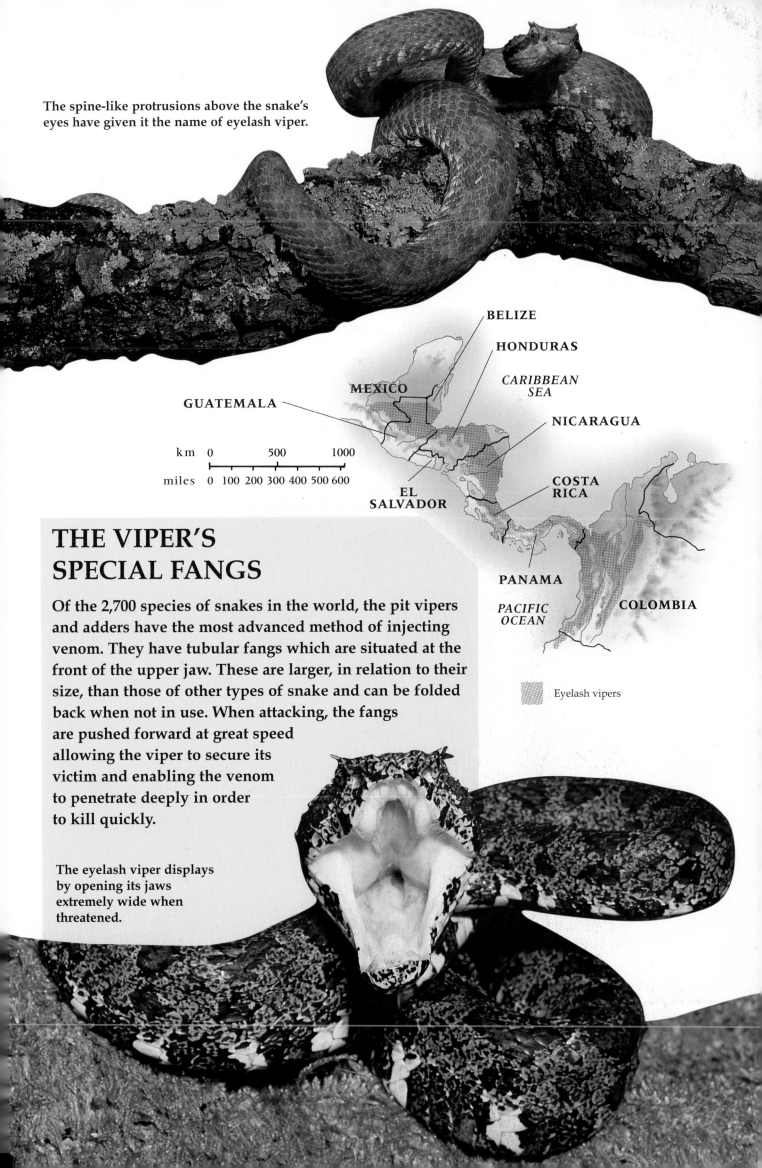

The spine-like protrusions above the snake's eyes have given it the name of eyelash viper.

BELIZE

HONDURAS

CARIBBEAN
SEA

MEXICO

GUATEMALA

NICARAGUA

km 0   500   1000

miles   0   100 200 300 400 500 600

COSTA
RICA

EL
SALVADOR

PANAMA

COLOMBIA

PACIFIC
OCEAN

Eyelash vipers

THE VIPER'S SPECIAL FANGS

Of the 2,700 species of snakes in the world, the pit vipers and adders have the most advanced method of injecting venom. They have tubular fangs which are situated at the front of the upper jaw. These are larger, in relation to their size, than those of other types of snake and can be folded back when not in use. When attacking, the fangs are pushed forward at great speed allowing the viper to secure its victim and enabling the venom to penetrate deeply in order to kill quickly.

The eyelash viper displays by opening its jaws extremely wide when threatened.

The Amazon Parrots of the Windward Isles

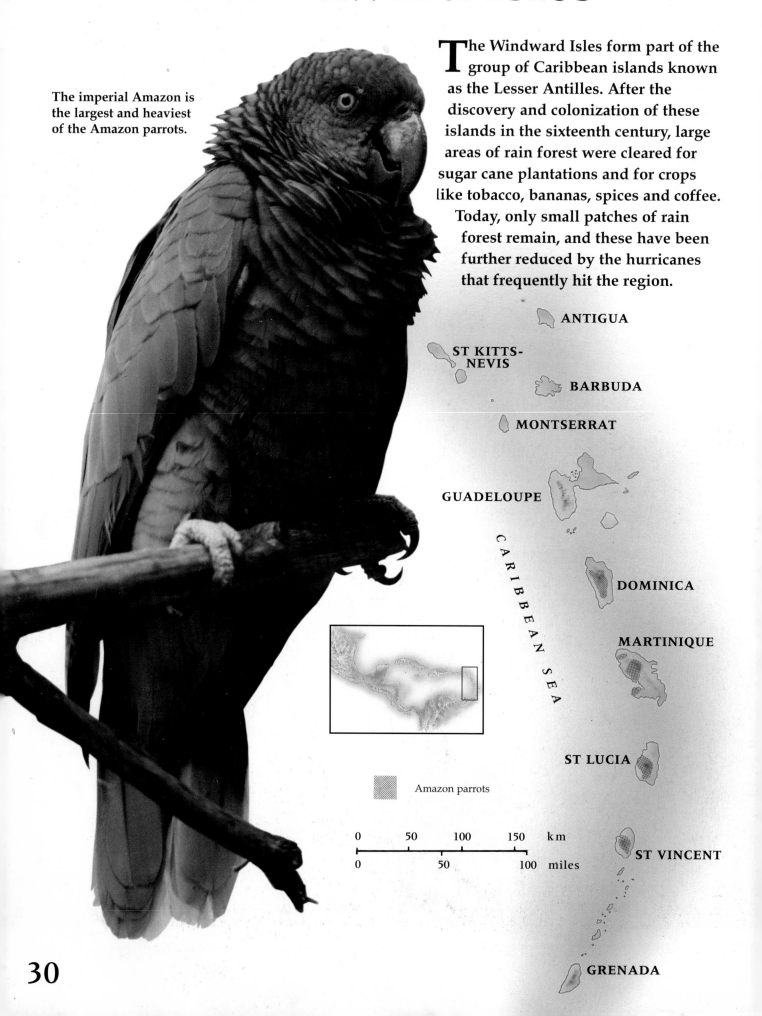

The imperial Amazon is the largest and heaviest of the Amazon parrots.

The Windward Isles form part of the group of Caribbean islands known as the Lesser Antilles. After the discovery and colonization of these islands in the sixteenth century, large areas of rain forest were cleared for sugar cane plantations and for crops like tobacco, bananas, spices and coffee. Today, only small patches of rain forest remain, and these have been further reduced by the hurricanes that frequently hit the region.

ANTIGUA

ST KITTS-NEVIS

BARBUDA

MONTSERRAT

GUADELOUPE

CARIBBEAN SEA

DOMINICA

MARTINIQUE

ST LUCIA

Amazon parrots

| 0 | 50 | 100 | 150 | km |
| 0 | | 50 | | 100 | miles |

ST VINCENT

GRENADA

Among the wildlife worst affected by forest destruction are the four species of Amazon parrot. Now internationally recognized as endangered, the rarest of these parrots is the imperial Amazon found only on the island of Dominica. In 1990 only 80 birds were believed to exist. Also native only to Dominica, the red-necked Amazon was estimated to number about 350 in 1990. Both these parrots were once widespread throughout the mountainous interior of the island. They have suffered a drastic reduction in numbers – especially in the last 50 years.

The St Vincent Amazon often feeds and roosts in flocks with 20–30 others.

The St Lucia Amazon and the St Vincent Amazon, found only on the islands of St Lucia and St Vincent respectively, have suffered similarly. The range of the St Lucia Amazon has now been reduced to about 65–70 square kilometres and only about 350 birds are thought to be left. The 500 or so St Vincent Amazons (estimated in the late 1980s) probably have less than 16 square kilometres of primary rain forest left to live in.

PARROTS AND THE PET TRADE

Alongside the destruction of their habitat, the trapping of Amazon parrots to supply the pet trade has been a major cause of their decline. International trade in all four species is now illegal, but trapping for foreign bird collectors continues to be a future threat. It is estimated that more than a million birds, many of them parrots, are imported into the European Union every year.

These parrots are being kept at a holding centre before being exported around the world.

SOUTH AMERICA

When we think of South American rain forests, it is usually the dense tropical forests of the Amazon river basin that come to mind. However, there are other distinct regions of tropical rain forest on the continent, as well as areas of temperate rain forest.

A third area of rain forest is found along the east coast of Brazil. Now reduced to a mere 1–5 per cent of its original size, this Atlantic forest exists only in small fragments. Luxuriant and tall, the forest is known to contain 2,124 species of butterflies and 17 primate species, including the endangered golden lion tamarin.

TROPICAL RAIN FORESTS

South America contains the world's largest expanse of tropical rain forest. It covers over 6 million sq km and is centred on the drainage basin of the Amazon river, though it spreads beyond this – notably into Venezuela and the Guianas in the north and into the foothills of the Andes mountains in the south-west.

Extending into nine different countries, but with 60 per cent in Brazil, the Amazon basin is a mixture of different environments. It includes wetlands (flooded forest), dry savanna areas and montane forests. There are probably more species of animal and plant here than anywhere else on earth: about 20 per cent of all flowering plant and possibly bird species, and about 10 per cent of the world's mammals. More than 370 indigenous Indian peoples live in the Amazon region.

A separate stretch of lowland rain forest, known as the Chocó, extends down from Central America to run along Colombia's coast. One of the world's wettest regions (in some places rainfall is over 10,000 mm each year), it is also immensely rich in plant and animal species, many of which – including over 100 birds – are found nowhere else.

Below **The three-toed sloth clings on to forest branches using its specialized claws.**

TEMPERATE RAIN FORESTS

Chile has the largest area of coastal temperate rain forest in the southern hemisphere. It contains trees such as the alerce, the monkey puzzle and southern beeches. In Argentina there are some small blocks of alpine rain forest in the Andes mountains and some temperate rain forest at the eastern end of Tierra del Fuego.

Temperate rain forests are evergreen and receive heavy rainfall, However, they have lower average temperatures and a smaller variety of animal and plant species than tropical rain forests.

Tropical rain forest extends high up the sides of the Sierra Parima mountain range in the Venezuelan Amazon.

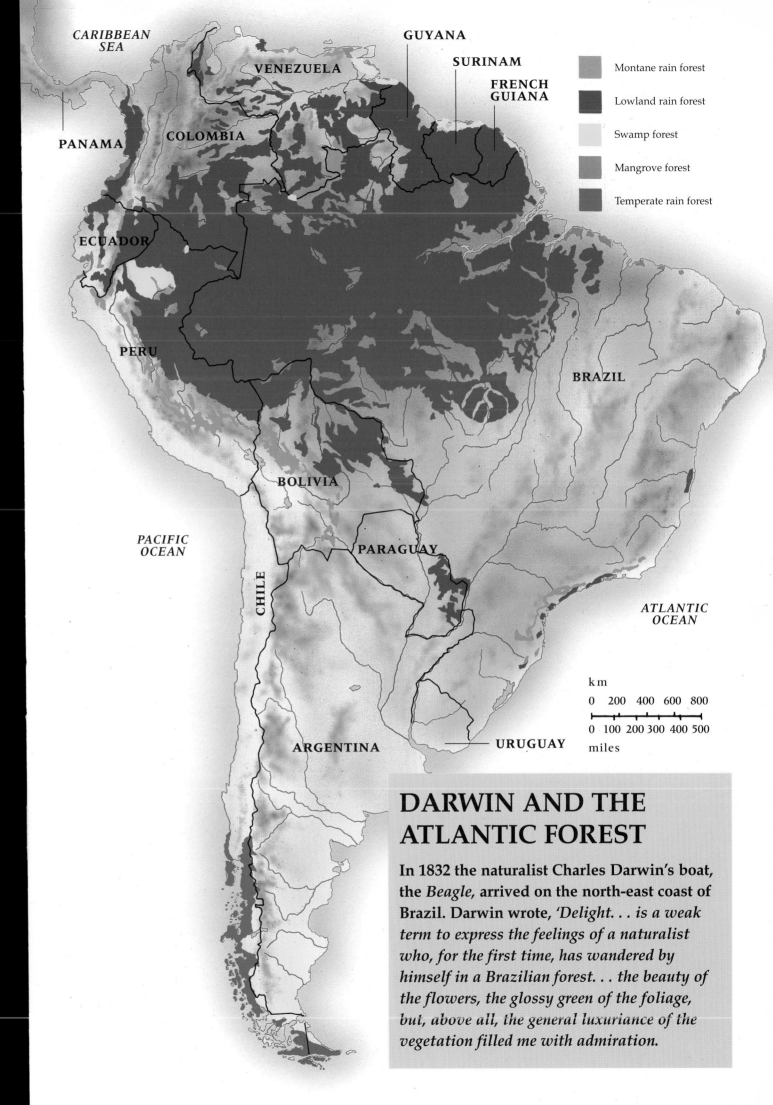

CARIBBEAN
SEA

GUYANA

VENEZUELA

SURINAM

FRENCH
GUIANA

PANAMA

COLOMBIA

Montane rain forest

Lowland rain forest

Swamp forest

Mangrove forest

Temperate rain forest

ECUADOR

PERU

BRAZIL

BOLIVIA

PACIFIC
OCEAN

PARAGUAY

CHILE

ATLANTIC
OCEAN

km

0 200 400 600 800

0 100 200 300 400 500

ARGENTINA

URUGUAY

miles

DARWIN AND THE ATLANTIC FOREST

In 1832 the naturalist Charles Darwin's boat,
the *Beagle*, arrived on the north-east coast of
Brazil. Darwin wrote, '*Delight. . . is a weak
term to express the feelings of a naturalist
who, for the first time, has wandered by
himself in a Brazilian forest. . . the beauty of
the flowers, the glossy green of the foliage,
but, above all, the general luxuriance of the
vegetation filled me with admiration.*

The Machiguenga

The Machiguenga are one of Peru's 60 indigenous peoples. They live in the south-east of the country along part of the Urubamba river – where montane rain forest covers the foothills of the Andes – and in the flatter, densely forested region to the east.

Because of the influence of missionaries, many Machiguenga now live in small, permanent villages. However, families traditionally lived either separately or in small clusters of houses, which would be abandoned when the families moved to different parts of the forest from time to time.

The Machiguenga hunt animals, catch fish and grow a large variety of crops in small gardens cleared in the forest. Their staple food is manioc – a starchy tuber, looking rather like a long potato – and they enjoy many different kinds.

0   50   100   150   km

0   50   100   miles

Rio Ucayali

PERU

Puiha

Shivankoreni

Rio Manu

Camisea

Tayakome

Mantaro

Diamante

Rio Apurímac

Shimaa

Chirumpia

Quillabamba

ANDES MOUNTAINS

Rio Urubamba

Rio Yavero

Machu Picchu

Cuzco

The Machiguenga

In the last thirty years much of the Machiguenga's territory has been taken over by colonists from other areas. Much of their forest has been cut down and planted with coffee and other cash crops. Many Machiguenga now grow coffee and cocoa crops themselves. By selling their produce they can buy some of the goods they want, such as metal items and Western clothes.

Machiguenga Indians trade plantains and sugar cane for salt with settlers.

THE KUGAPAKORI

A number of Machiguenga – known as the Kugapakori – have not yet been contacted by Westerners. They are believed to live in the remote forests in and around the region of the Manu National Park. Gold miners have recently entered part of the region in large numbers, as well as teams of people exploring for oil and gas. How long the Kugapakori will be able to continue living in isolation is uncertain.

Above A Machiguenga girl spins cotton that will be used to make a traditional cushma.

The traditional outfit worn by Machiguenga men and women is the cushma. This is a long tunic woven by the women from cotton grown in their gardens. It is coloured brown with vegetable dyes.

A Machiguenga settlement in a clearing of the forest. The houses have roofs made of palm thatch.

The Mamirauá Flooded Forest

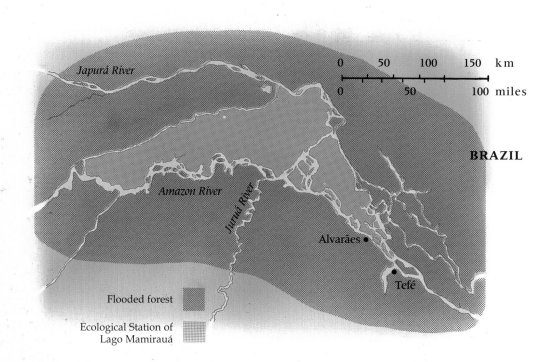

BRAZIL

Flooded forest

Ecological Station of
Lago Mamirauá

Right (main picture) A *caboclo* boy fishing with a spear in the flooded forest in Brazil.

Across the Amazon region, large areas of forest that border the Amazon river itself and some of its tributaries become flooded for part of each year. One of the most fascinating and least disturbed of these areas is the Mamirauá, in the Brazilian state of Amazonas, 600 km upstream from the Amazon port of Manaus.

From March to August each year the water level rises by up to 15 m, flooding the area completely and leaving only the tallest trees visible above the surface of the water. The lower branches, which during the dry season are home to monkeys, birds and reptiles, become the hunting ground for the Amazonian pink dolphin and the spawning grounds for more than 2,000 species of fish. These include the giant pirarucu and tambaqui which eat the fruit and seeds of forest trees.

The forest is home to some of the world's most endangered animals and birds. These include the white uakari, the recently discovered blackish squirrel monkey, the umbrella bird, the black caiman and the freshwater manatee. A large part of this region now forms part of the Ecological Station of Lago Mamirauá, which covers an area of nearly 1.2 million ha and is the world's largest protected area of flooded forest.

Flooded-forest villagers peeling manioc, their staple food crop.

Right (inset picture) Tambaqui fish swim among the branches of flooded-forest trees in search of fruit and seeds that fall into the water.

THE *CABOCLOS* OF THE FLOODED FOREST

The flooded forest is also the home of *caboclos*. These are people who have lived in the rain forest for generations. They make use of the forest and its extraordinary change in water levels very much like the Amerindians from whom they are partly descended. For example, they net or harpoon fish that become trapped in isolated lakes as the floodwaters recede and harvest their staple crop, manioc, from their silt-rich gardens before the floodwaters cover them.

The Brazil Nut Tree

Brazil nut trees are native to the Amazon rain forest and are scattered across almost the entire region. Mature trees can grow to a height of over 60 m and live for over 1,000 years. They have a majestic appearance and their straight trunks are free of branches for two thirds of their height. Brazil nut trees are generally found growing with other large tree species.

It is thought that Amazonian Indian peoples introduced Brazil nut trees to many areas of the rain forest, in order to harvest their nutritious nuts. But a forest rodent, the agouti, also plays an important part in their dispersal. Between 15 and 24 Brazil nuts form inside the large, round, woody fruits or pods (weighing up to 1.5 kg each) produced by the female trees. When they fall to the ground the agouti chews through the pods and will often bury hoards of nuts in different places, sometimes as far as 46 m away from the mother tree. Although many nuts are dug up and eaten by agoutis and other animals, some seeds germinate to form new trees.

All the Brazil nuts we eat are gathered from the wild, often by Amazonian Indians. It is a hazardous job because the heavy pods, falling from high up, can kill a person standing under the tree. Once collected, the pods are all cracked open by hand.

BEES, ORCHIDS AND BRAZIL NUTS

Brazil nut trees only produce nuts when they grow in the wild, and not in plantations. This is because their life cycle is very complex. Female trees produce large yellow flowers and these are pollinated only by female orchid bees which come visiting in search of nectar. The male bees gather the scent produced by a particular rain forest orchid to attract the females to mate. If the forest around a Brazil nut tree is burnt or felled, the bees and orchids are also destroyed and its flowers will not be pollinated.

VENEZUELA
GUYANA
SURINAM
FRENCH
GUIANA

ATLANTIC
OCEAN

Boa Vista

ECUADOR

Obidos

Manaus

Belém

Amazon River

Iquitos

PACIFIC OCEAN

Porto Velho

BRAZIL

PERU

BOLIVIA

Brazil nut trees

0   500   1000   1500   km

0   200   400   600   800   miles

Above A *caboclo* man cracks open
a Brazil nut pod with a machete.

Main picture Brazil nut trees on
the Amazonian skyline.

The Goliath Bird-Eating Spider

A Goliath bird-eating spider eating a snake in its underground burrow.

The world's largest spider is the Goliath bird-eating spider. It is one of approximately 300 bird-eating spiders in the world, which are also sometimes called tarantulas. Its body can grow to about 9 cm long and its leg span to 26 cm.

While bird-eating spiders – which are mostly forest-dwelling – are found throughout the tropics and subtropics, the Goliath bird-eating spider is native to the rain forests of northern South America, being found in Surinam, Guyana, Venezuela and Brazil. It is an extremely bold and aggressive spider, living in burrows in the ground, and hunting on the forest floor. Other bird-eating spiders may live under stones, bark or leaf litter or above the ground in trees.

Bird-eating spiders can have bright colouration like the Bolivian *Pamphobetus antinous*, which has a purple sheen, and the Mexican red-kneed tarantula. The Goliath bird-eating spider varies in colour from black to a rich red-brown. All are thickly covered with hairs which make them very sensitive to vibrations. Although they may occasionally catch small birds or mammals such as mice, these spiders generally prey on small reptiles and amphibians, like frogs and toads, beetles, moths, grasshoppers and other spiders. Since many other forest animals will eat them, the spiders feed mainly at night.

Right A fledgling bird being eaten by a bird-eating spider.

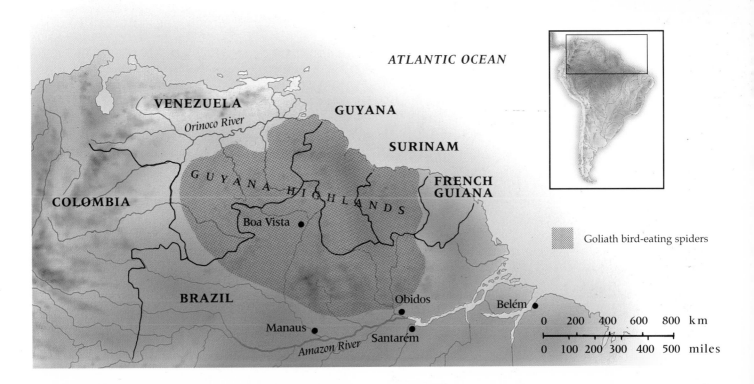

ATLANTIC OCEAN

VENEZUELA
GUYANA
Orinoco River
SURINAM
COLOMBIA
FRENCH
GUIANA
GUYANA HIGHLANDS
Boa Vista
Goliath bird-eating spiders
BRAZIL
Obidos
Belém
Manaus
0   200   400   600   800   k m
Santarém
Amazon River
0   100 200 300 400 500   miles

Above A Goliath bird-eating spider raises its two front legs and shows its fangs to defend itself.

HOW BIRD-EATING SPIDERS KILL

To overpower their prey, bird-eating spiders raise their front legs and the front half of their body and then strike downward with their large parallel fangs, injecting a lethal poison. Spiders can only eat liquid food, so their venom breaks down the internal organs of their prey allowing the spider to suck it dry. Although a bird-eating spider's bite can be painful, it is not usually fatal to people.

The Jaguar

The jaguar is the largest species of the cat family in the Americas. Up to 2.5 m long, including its tail, the jaguar can weigh as much as 140 kg. Despite its heavy build, the jaguar's movements are rapid and agile and it is an excellent climber.

The background colour of the jaguar's coat can vary greatly, but the typical colouration is an orange-tan marked with black spots arranged in rosettes with smaller black spots in the centre. This dappled coat blends perfectly with the light and shadows falling on the forest floor as the foliage moves above.

At the beginning of this century the jaguar's territory extended from the south-western United States down to the Rio Negro in Argentina. Today, this area has become smaller, extending from central Mexico to northern Argentina.

Although the animals are also found in thorn scrub and dry deciduous forest, their rain-forest habitat has been greatly reduced by ranching, agriculture, logging and colonization.

The jaguar is a solitary animal. It very rarely attacks people, but preys on all the larger mammals in the forest including tapirs and brocket deer. Jaguars are excellent swimmers and can often be found near rivers, where they may catch turtles, otters or capybaras. They also eat fish. The jaguar can attract fish by dangling its tail in the water as a lure.

Water-loving animals, such as capybaras, are sometimes caught by jaguars. This capybara sitting on a river bank in Brazil's Mato Grosso region is surrounded by spectacled caimans.

USA

ATLANTIC
OCEAN

MEXICO

BELIZE

HONDURAS

PACIFIC
OCEAN

VENEZUELA

PANAMA

GUYANA

GUATEMALA

SURINAM

EL SALVADOR

FRENCH
GUIANA

NICARAGUA

COLOMBIA

COSTA RICA

ECUADOR

BRAZIL

PERU

BOLIVIA

PARAGUAY

ARGENTINA

Jaguars

| 0 | 1000 | 2000 | 3000 | km |
| 0 | 500 | 1000 | 1500 | 2000 | miles |

42

JAGUARS AND THE SKIN TRADE

Now very rare, the jaguar has been exterminated in many areas through continuous hunting and trapping for skins and trophies. It is already thought to be extinct in El Salvador, Uruguay and Chile, and faces extinction in Argentina, Costa Rica and Panama. Although jaguars are now legally protected throughout their range, except in Mexico and Belize, and are internationally recognized as endangered, they continue to be hunted and trapped.

Above left Jaguar and black panther skins and heads are still on sale in some South American countries.

A jaguar rests between meals in the branches of a tree in the Brazilian Pantanal wetland.

The Alerce

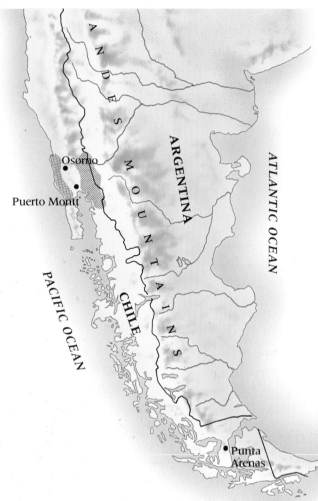

Alerce forest

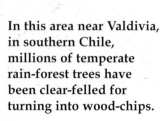

Southern Chile has a temperate wet oceanic climate, with very heavy rainfall each year – usually between 1,500 and 4,000 mm. It is here that a quarter of all the temperate rain forest in the world is now found.

Perhaps the most remarkable and most endangered of Chile's rain forest trees (which are almost entirely evergreen) is the alerce conifer. It is sometimes called the giant redwood of South America, and is the second longest-living tree in the world, after the bristlecone pine. It can reach heights of up to 70 m and a diameter of over 4 m, and is extremely slow-growing. A tree cut down in 1975 was shown by its growth rings to have been over 3,600 years old, but today almost all the most ancient trees have been felled or burnt.

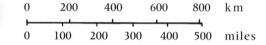

| 0 | 200 | 400 | 600 | 800 | k m |
| 0 | 100 | 200 | 300 | 400 | 500 | miles |

In this area near Valdivia, in southern Chile, millions of temperate rain-forest trees have been clear-felled for turning into wood-chips.

Two distinct populations of alerce remain in Chile: one along the coastal mountains and the other along the Andes. In each of these forest areas a range of associated trees and shrubs is also found. Alerce forests once covered a large area, stretching from the southern Chilean coast to the Andes and over the border into Argentina. Although trees can still be seen within this area their numbers are now so few that the species is endangered and international trade in its timber is banned. However, the toughness and extremely straight grain of alerce timber has made it highly sought after, and logging is still occuring illegally.

Right **This ranger is guarding the oldest remaining alerce tree.**

THE LAST GIANT ALERCE

Near Valdivia in southern Chile the Alerce National Monument reserve has been created to help protect possibly the largest and oldest remaining alerce tree. This tree has a circumference of 13 m and is thought to be about 1,000 years old. Park rangers are guarding the tree as it is one of the last truly giant alerce trees left.

AFRICA

The rain forests of Africa now cover only 7 per cent of the continent and make up slightly less than a fifth of all the rain forest on earth. Although the rain forests contain more than half of Africa's animal and plant species, they are not as rich in species as the other main rain forest areas of Southeast Asia and Latin America. Africa's rain forests include dense evergreen lowland forest, cool montane forest, swamp forest and coastal mangrove forest.

The evergreen lowland forests and swamp forests cover the largest area and have the greatest variety of plants and animals. The vast Central African rain forests, for example, have more than 1,100 species of butterflies, 40 kinds of monkey and over 8,000 species of plants. This area is also home to African elephants and buffalos, and to okapis, which are found nowhere else.

The mangrove and montane forests cover a much smaller area but contain some of the world's rarest animals and plants. Many of the plants and animals found in the cool montane forest are now endangered and found in very restricted areas. These include the mountain gorilla and 26 species of meat-eating snails. The mangrove forests are important as the breeding grounds for many types of sea and estuarine fish, such as mud skippers.

The island of Madagascar has many animals and plants that are unique. These include species of lemur, the aye-aye and many kinds of medicinal plant. Today, only a fraction of Madagascar's eastern coastal rain forest remains, but it is still one of the world's richest areas for plants.

BUSH MEAT

A great variety of wild foods are eaten by the peoples who live in and around Africa's rain forests. In West Africa, up to one fifth of all animal protein eaten in rural areas is hunted or gathered directly from the forest. Usually referred to as bush meat, the foods include a variety of monkeys, small antelopes, porcupines, cane rats, caterpillars, termites and the giant African land snail. The rapid rise in the population of countries like Nigeria, has led to increased hunting pressures on many rare animals.

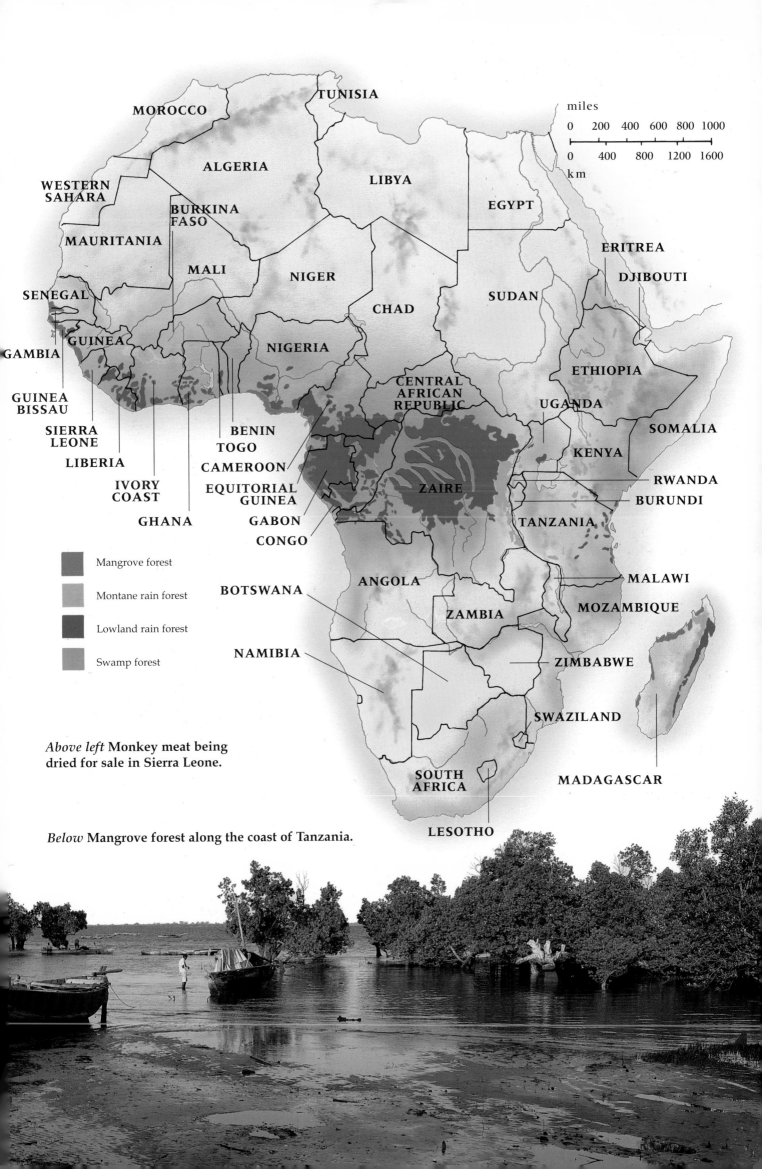

MOROCCO

TUNISIA

ALGERIA

LIBYA

WESTERN
SAHARA

EGYPT

BURKINA
FASO

MAURITANIA

MALI

NIGER

CHAD

SUDAN

ERITREA

DJIBOUTI

SENEGAL

ETHIOPIA

GAMBIA

GUINEA

NIGERIA

GUINEA
BISSAU

CENTRAL
AFRICAN
REPUBLIC

UGANDA

SOMALIA

SIERRA
LEONE

BENIN

KENYA

LIBERIA

TOGO

CAMEROON

ZAIRE

RWANDA

IVORY
COAST

EQUITORIAL
GUINEA

BURUNDI

GHANA

GABON

TANZANIA

CONGO

BOTSWANA

ANGOLA

MALAWI

MOZAMBIQUE

NAMIBIA

ZAMBIA

ZIMBABWE

miles

0   200 400 600 800 1000

0   400 800 1200 1600

km

Mangrove forest

Montane rain forest

Lowland rain forest

Swamp forest

SWAZILAND

MADAGASCAR

SOUTH
AFRICA

LESOTHO

Above left Monkey meat being
dried for sale in Sierra Leone.

Below Mangrove forest along the coast of Tanzania.

The Baka

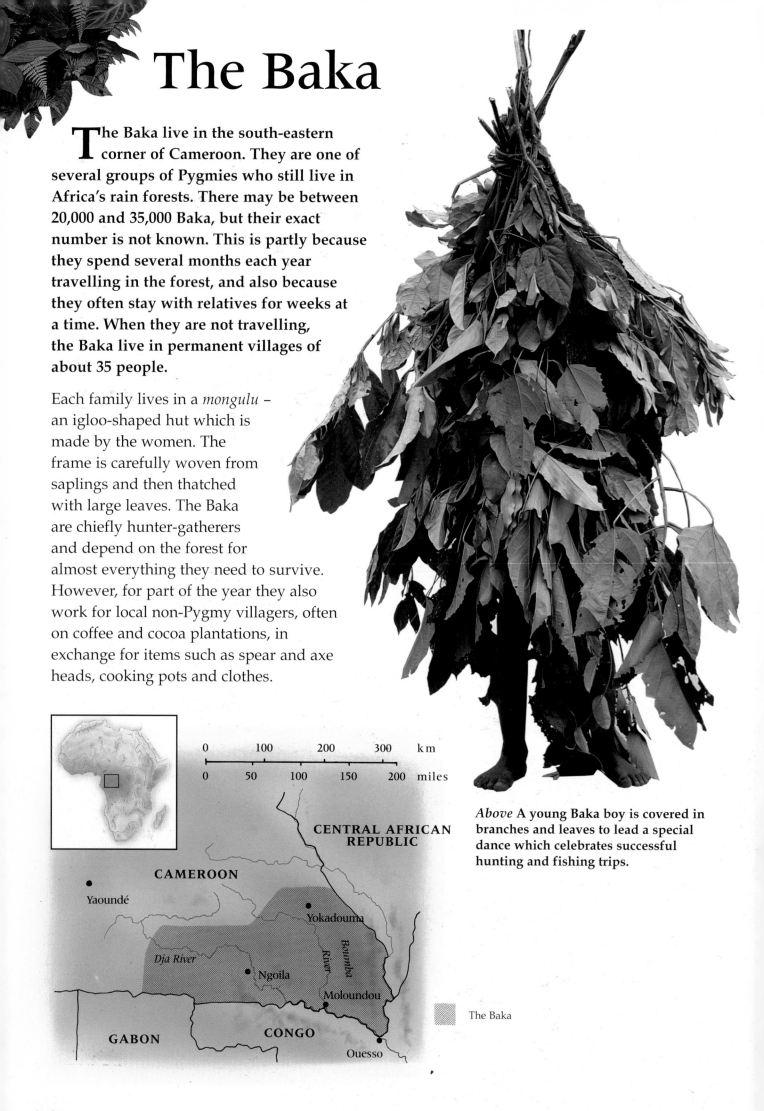

The Baka live in the south-eastern corner of Cameroon. They are one of several groups of Pygmies who still live in Africa's rain forests. There may be between 20,000 and 35,000 Baka, but their exact number is not known. This is partly because they spend several months each year travelling in the forest, and also because they often stay with relatives for weeks at a time. When they are not travelling, the Baka live in permanent villages of about 35 people.

Each family lives in a *mongulu* – an igloo-shaped hut which is made by the women. The frame is carefully woven from saplings and then thatched with large leaves. The Baka are chiefly hunter-gatherers and depend on the forest for almost everything they need to survive. However, for part of the year they also work for local non-Pygmy villagers, often on coffee and cocoa plantations, in exchange for items such as spear and axe heads, cooking pots and clothes.

Above A young Baka boy is covered in branches and leaves to lead a special dance which celebrates successful hunting and fishing trips.

0	100	200	300	k m
0	50	100	150	200	miles

CENTRAL AFRICAN REPUBLIC

CAMEROON

Yaoundé

Yokadouma

Dja River

Baumba River

Ngoila

Moloundou

GABON

CONGO

Ouesso

The Baka

The Baka are extremely skilful at using the forest, and know exactly when and where to find wild plants for medicines, as well as foods. In addition to fish, game and fruit, the foods they gather include many kinds of edible roots and yams, about twenty species of edible mushroom, beetle larvae, caterpillars and, best-loved of all, several kinds of honey.

Above Baka villagers outside their *mongulu* huts. Women, in particular, often spend much of their time together.

FRUITS FROM THE FOREST

During the three-month rainy season the Baka leave their permanent villages to hunt and gather deep in the forest, building temporary camps as they go. At this time many trees produce their fruit, attracting animals and people alike. One of the fruits most enjoyed by the Baka is the wild mango. Underneath its juicy yellow flesh the kernel contains a rich oil which makes an important addition to their diet.

Baka pygmies, using a large forest leaf as a work surface, are cutting up a tortoise they have caught to eat.

49

The Aye-Aye

Red-bellied lemurs eating flowers.

The aye-aye is one of the thirty species of lemur that are found only on the island of Madagascar. Lemurs have long bushy tails, which they use to help them balance as they leap from branch to branch or when they are sitting eating.

The aye-aye spends most of its time on its own and is rarely seen with others. Unlike most other mammals it builds a nest, often in the fork of a tall tree, and spends much of the day curled up asleep inside it. When it wakes up at dusk, however, it is very energetic. The aye-aye is an excellent climber and can hang from the branches by its hind legs. It ventures down from the trees from time to time and scampers across the forest floor with its tail in the air. Aye-ayes feed at night on insect larvae, and also on coconuts – which they crack open with their powerful teeth – sugar cane, giant bamboo, lychees and mangos, as well as other nuts and seeds.

No one knows how many aye-ayes are left in Madagascar today. Almost all the lowland forest has been cut down and only a fraction of the country's original rain forest survives. Aye-ayes are thought to be widely, but very thinly, scattered among this remaining forest.

An aye-aye gnawing through the outer skin of a coconut, one of its favourite foods.

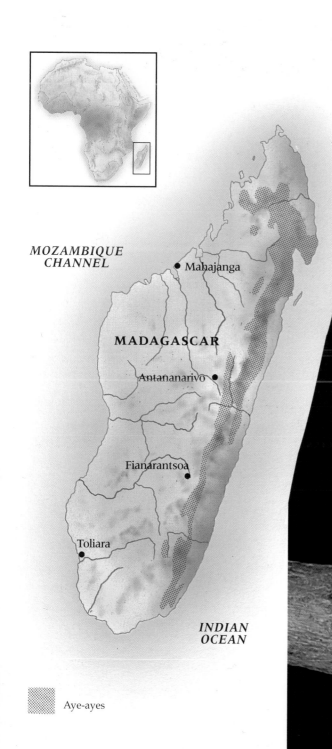

MOZAMBIQUE
CHANNEL

MADAGASCAR

INDIAN
OCEAN

Aye-ayes

| 0 | 100 | 200 | 300 | 400 | 500 km |
| 0 | | 100 | 200 | | 300 miles |

THE AYE-AYE'S SPECIAL HANDS

The aye-aye has developed a curious feature which makes it different from all the other lemurs. This is an extra-thin, bony third finger on each of its front paws, with a special second joint allowing the finger to be turned in any direction. When searching for larvae the aye-aye taps this finger against a tree trunk or branch to try and detect insect tunnels inside. When the aye-aye finds a tunnel it bites away the bark, and twists its bony finger inside to pull out the grub.

The African Mahogany

African mahogany is the name given to timber produced by five similar species of tree growing in the rain forests of West and Central Africa. One of these is *Khaya ivorensis*. It is a magnificent tree – one of the great rain forest giants – and is spread widely throughout the rain forests of West and Central Africa. The tree grows up to 60 m in height and reaches 1.8 m in diameter. It has a straight trunk, which is free of branches for up to 27 m and is supported by short buttress roots at its base. The timber, which is a reddish brown in colour and sometimes has a decorative stripe running through it, is exported for use in furniture and boat-building.

The timber from a variety of different rain forest trees around the world is called mahogany. These include trees from South and Central America, Australia and Southeast Asia. African mahogany is often used as a substitute for South American mahogany, which is now seriously endangered.

Other African mahoganies (which are other *Khaya* species) are found from Guinea-Bissau to Angola and from Sudan to Mozambique. The timber of unrelated sapele trees is sometimes traded as mahogany.

A large African mahogany tree is cut into sections with a chainsaw.

LOGGING FOR MAHOGANY

Much of the African mahogany being traded today comes from the Côte D'Ivoire, Ghana, Gabon, Cameroon and Nigeria. Although some of these countries' forest reserves are thought to be well-managed, in most cases the forests in which mahogany trees grow are being cleared in an uncontrolled way. As a result, mahogany trees are now threatened. Despite this, a variety of familiar items – including doors and toilet seats – are still being made from the wood.

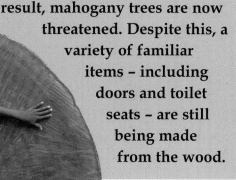

A Nigerian boy in front of a log. Nigeria has been earning millions of dollars each year from logging, but less than 10 per cent of its intact rain forest remains.

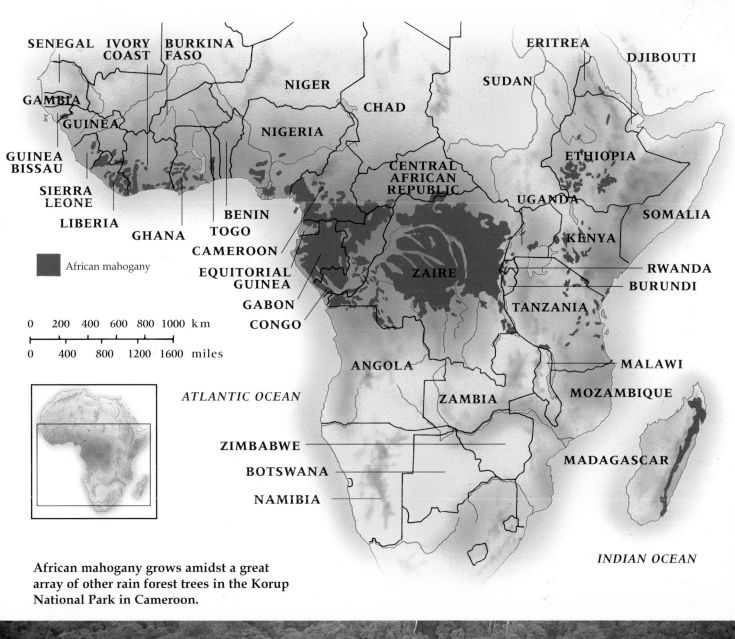

SENEGAL IVORY BURKINA ERITREA DJIBOUTI
COAST FASO
GAMBIA NIGER SUDAN
GUINEA CHAD
NIGERIA
GUINEA
BISSAU ETHIOPIA
SIERRA CENTRAL
LEONE AFRICAN
REPUBLIC UGANDA
LIBERIA BENIN SOMALIA
GHANA TOGO KENYA
CAMEROON ZAIRE RWANDA
EQUITORIAL BURUNDI
GUINEA TANZANIA
GABON
CONGO
ANGOLA MALAWI
MOZAMBIQUE
ZAMBIA
ZIMBABWE MADAGASCAR
BOTSWANA
NAMIBIA

African mahogany

ATLANTIC OCEAN

INDIAN OCEAN

0   200   400   600   800 1000 km
0   400   800 1200 1600 miles

African mahogany grows amidst a great
array of other rain forest trees in the Korup
National Park in Cameroon.

The Mountain Gorilla

Three different kinds of gorilla live in Africa's tropical forests. The Western lowland gorilla is the most numerous and can be found over a relatively wide range in West Africa. The Eastern lowland gorilla, by contrast, lives only in eastern Zaire. The most endangered of the three is the mountain gorilla, which is found only in the region of the Virunga volcanoes, on the borders of Rwanda, Zaire, and Uganda – mainly in three protected areas – and in the Bwindi-Impenetrable National Park of south-west Uganda.

Park guards with a silver back mountain gorilla in the Virunga National Park, Zaire.

The montane forests that are home to the mountain gorilla are cool, damp and often shrouded in mist. Many of the trees and rocks are covered in thick moss. The gorillas live on the forest floor, but climb into tree branches to make nests at night. Mountain gorillas are entirely vegetarian. They feed on the leaves, shoots and juicy stems of plants, such as bamboos, that form the forest undergrowth, and on fruit.

Mountain gorillas are very sociable animals. They live in family groups of 10 or so individuals; several family groups will share the same piece of forest peacefully. Grooming one another plays a very important role in the lives of mountain gorillas, relaxing them as well as strengthening the bonds between group members.

A female gorilla with her baby in a rain forest in Rwanda. A young gorilla stays with its mother for about three years after it is born.

Opposite This group of local people has gathered to see the body of a mountain gorilla that has been killed by poachers in Rwanda.

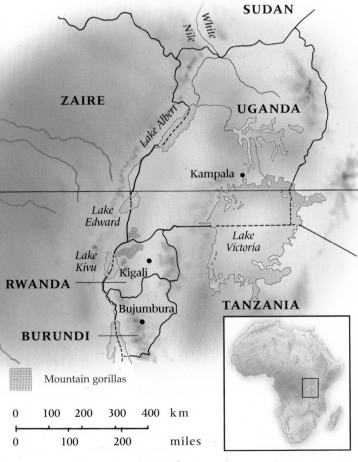

Mountain gorillas

| 0 | 100 | 200 | 300 | 400 | k m |

| 0 | | 100 | | 200 | | miles |

THE DISAPPEARING GORILLAS

Mountain gorillas have been widely hunted for food and sport, and by collectors who shoot females in order to take their young. Today, only 650 are believed to be left in the wild and all international trade is banned. Despite being protected by law, mountain gorillas are still being killed by poachers. Many are injured or killed by traps and snares set for other animals. The continuing destruction of their forest habitat is another serious threat to their existence.

The African Oil Palm

West Africa's people have used the African oil palm tree for thousands of years. It is native to the rain forests of West Africa, where large numbers of wild trees often grow together forming groves. Mature trees can reach 17 m in height and produce large fruit bunches consisting of up to two hundred individual fruits. These fruits, each about 2.5 cm long, are most often a red-orange in colour.

The fruits are unusual because they contain two different kinds of oil. Palm oil is the name of the oil which is pressed from the fleshy outer part of the fruits. It has many commercial uses but is particularly important in the manufacture of soap, shampoo and cosmetics. Palm kernel oil is pressed from the inner, nut-like kernels. It is widely used to make margarine and is found in many processed foods.

Left This man is high up in an oil palm tree collecting sap from the tree to make palm wine.

PALM WINE

The African oil palm has played an important part in traditional societies in West Africa, both as a food and as a drink. In Cameroon, palm wine is made simply by collecting the sap, overnight, from a partially felled palm. In the morning the palm wine is sweet, non-alcoholic and an excellent source of energy for the day ahead. By the evening the wine has fermented a little, is sour, and is drunk by the elders of the village in much the same way as beer in North America or Europe.

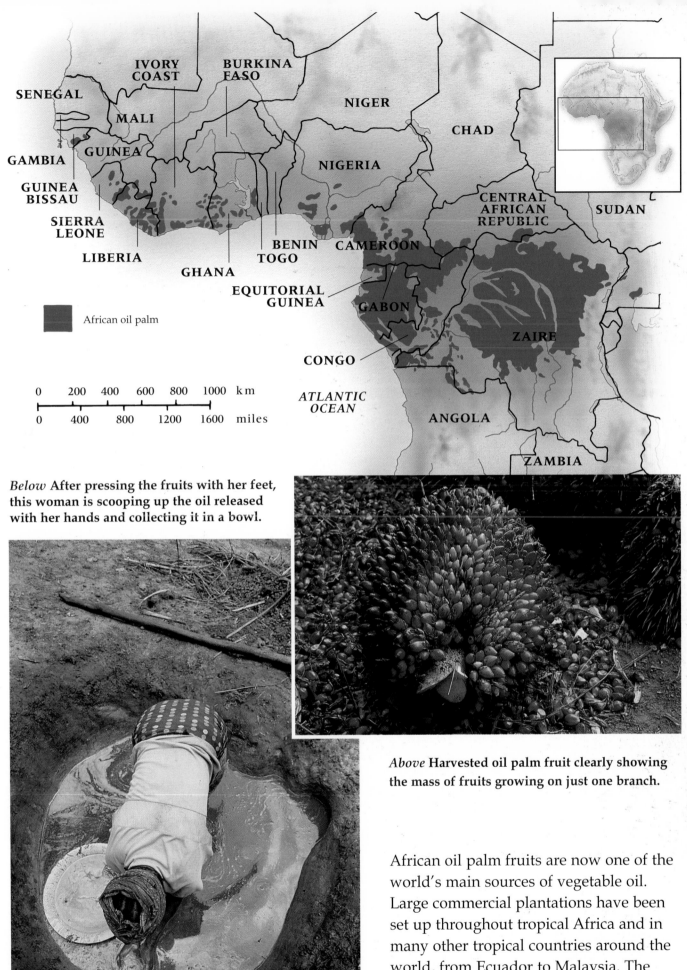

African oil palm

| 0 | 200 | 400 | 600 | 800 | 1000 | k m |

| 0 | 400 | 800 | 1200 | 1600 | miles |

Below After pressing the fruits with her feet, this woman is scooping up the oil released with her hands and collecting it in a bowl.

Above Harvested oil palm fruit clearly showing the mass of fruits growing on just one branch.

African oil palm fruits are now one of the world's main sources of vegetable oil. Large commercial plantations have been set up throughout tropical Africa and in many other tropical countries around the world, from Ecuador to Malaysia. The palm thrives only where rainfall is high, but can grow on poor soils. In some tropical countries, indigenous peoples have had their forests cut down to make way for oil palm plantations.

57

MAINLAND ASIA

In mainland Asia rain forests and seasonal monsoon forests are found from India in the west to Vietnam in the east. However, in recent decades large areas of forest have been cut down to make way for rice paddies and plantations of cash crops or logged for valuable timber. This has left the forests greatly fragmented and many of their animals and plants have become very rare. In India's Western Ghats, for example, the wild dog, sloth bear, tiger, mugger crocodile and the gaur (a rare cattle species), are all endangered due to habitat loss.

In Bangladesh less than 5 per cent of the country's rain and monsoon forest survives. The largest area is a vast coastal mangrove forest, the Sundurbans, where tigers can still be found. Further east, Thailand has only 15 per cent of its original rain forest – largely due to logging – and Myanmar has now become a major source of teak and other tropical hardwoods. In Cambodia and Vietnam large areas of forest were destroyed by bombing during the Vietnam War (1954–75) but the region still contains Asian elephants, Javan rhinos and the kouprey, another rare cattle species.

To the north, patches of rain forest extend into southern China. Here, and further west along this northern boundary, the rain forests gradually change into subtropical and then temperate rain forests but the limits of each have not been clearly defined.

People have been living in Asia for about one million years and many types of domesticated animals and plants originated there. The forests are still home to a large number of indigenous peoples, but their unique ways of life are increasingly threatened by modern development.

Tigers are now very rare in India, and a number of reserves have been set up to try to help protect them.

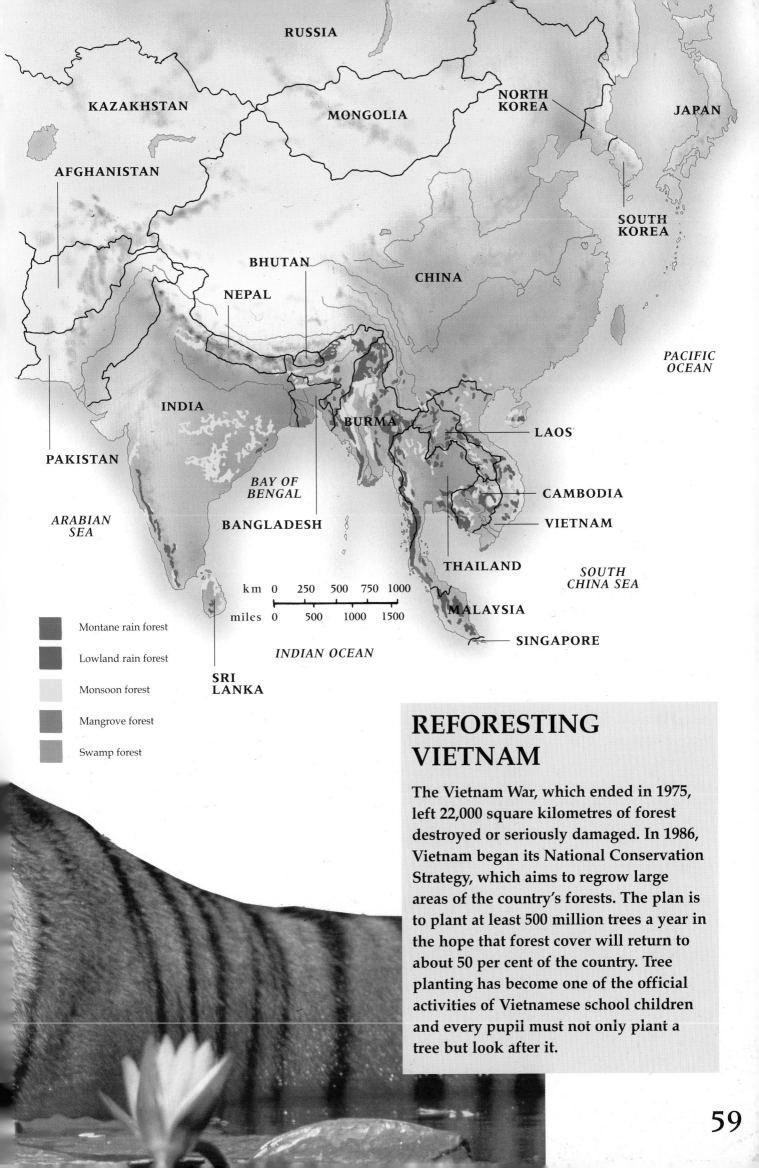

RUSSIA

KAZAKHSTAN

MONGOLIA

NORTH
KOREA

JAPAN

AFGHANISTAN

CHINA

SOUTH
KOREA

BHUTAN

NEPAL

PACIFIC
OCEAN

INDIA

BURMA

LAOS

PAKISTAN

BAY OF
BENGAL

CAMBODIA

VIETNAM

ARABIAN
SEA

BANGLADESH

THAILAND

SOUTH
CHINA SEA

km   0   250   500   750   1000

miles   0   500   1000   1500

MALAYSIA

Montane rain forest

Lowland rain forest

Monsoon forest

Mangrove forest

Swamp forest

SINGAPORE

INDIAN OCEAN

SRI
LANKA

REFORESTING VIETNAM

The Vietnam War, which ended in 1975, left 22,000 square kilometres of forest destroyed or seriously damaged. In 1986, Vietnam began its National Conservation Strategy, which aims to regrow large areas of the country's forests. The plan is to plant at least 500 million trees a year in the hope that forest cover will return to about 50 per cent of the country. Tree planting has become one of the official activities of Vietnamese school children and every pupil must not only plant a tree but look after it.

The Nayaka

About 1,400 Nayaka people live in the south-western foothills of the Nilgiris – a hilly plateau also known as the Blue Mountains – in the southern Indian state of Tamil Nadu and the adjoining parts of Kerala. This diverse region has many different types of forest, including lowland evergreen, montane *shola* forest and bamboo forest.

The Nayaka live in an area known as the Wynaad, in small communities made up of between one and five huts. The huts are built in forest clearings. They are sometimes made from strips of flattened bamboo and have roofs thatched with grass. The Nayaka move to a new part of the forest and build new huts every 6 to 18 months. They gather much of the food they need from the forest, including birds' eggs, wild yams and honey – a favourite food. The Nayaka also fish and hunt animals, and gather firewood and building materials from the forest. They sometimes spend one or more days on gathering expeditions, always carrying a woven basket, a curved knife for cutting vegetation and digging stick with them. Sometimes they spend the night in a cave.

The Nayaka trade forest produce with other people in the region, and wear shop-bought clothes. Some work on the large rubber, tea and coffee plantations that have been set up in their area, but they believe that they must try and live in the way that their ancestors did.

One group of Nayaka, called the Sholanayaka, make their homes in caves and live mainly by hunting, gathering and fishing. Once a year a special celebration is held and offerings are made to the spirits who control their lives.

HEALERS AND MAGICIANS

The Nayaka are regarded by others in the Nilgiris as having special supernatural powers and medicinal skills. Because of this they are generally feared, but are sought after for special cures and ritual objects they can find in the forest. Nayaka shamans are also believed to be able to bring prosperity and success.

The Sholanayaka are one of several different tribal peoples who live in the Nilgiri region.

A Sholanayaka family at the entrance to their cave.

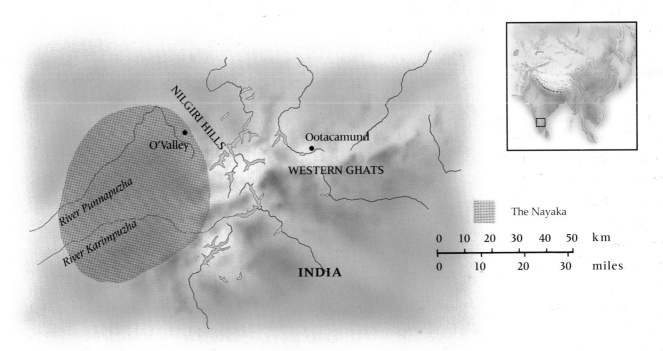

Much of the original forest of the Nilgiri Hills has been cleared for coffee and tea plantations.

The Xishuangbanna Nature Reserves

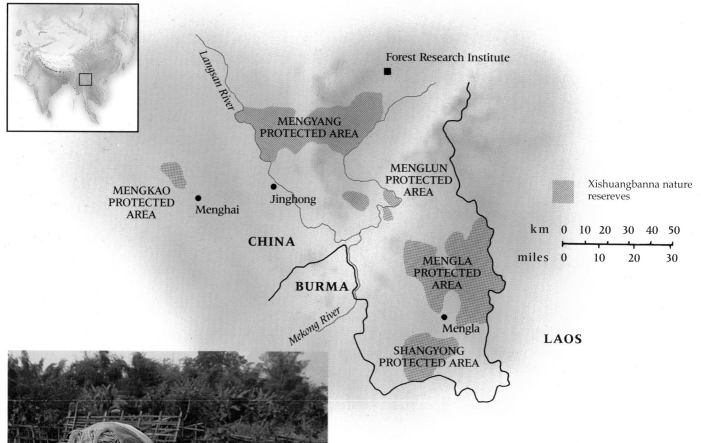

A Xishuangbanna farmer with baskets full of harvested food. A good water supply from unspoilt rain forest means that crops grow well.

Most of China's rain forest is situated in the southern province of Yunnan. In the prefecture of Xishuangbanna, five nature reserves have been created, covering an area of 242,000 ha. These reserves include some of the richest habitats in China, in terms of the variety of plants and animals they contain. The vegetation is very varied and includes evergreen, semi-evergreen, montane, monsoon and bamboo forests.

Although Xishuangbanna makes up only 0.2 per cent of China, 410 species of birds have been recorded, which is more than 35 per cent of the total for the whole of the country. The birds include the green peacock, silver pheasant, colourful sunbirds and flowerpeckers. Almost a quarter of China's mammal species are found here too, including the Asian elephant, tiger, clouded leopard and concolor gibbon, but many of these are now endangered.

Fork-tailed sunbirds are one of the 410 bird species found in Xishuangbanna.

The Xishuangbanna nature reserves contain 93 villages. Their population is having an increasing effect on the forests, because many people rely on them for products such as game and medicinal plants such as wild ginger. Since the 1950s the number of people in the Yunnan area has doubled and over the last 20 years half of Yunnan's forests have been cut down. In Xishuangbanna the Chinese government intends to turn more forest areas into tea and rubber plantations and to develop the region in general. This means that the reserves will now have to be carefully managed to protect their animals and plants.

THE FRAGILE FOREST

The forests of Xishuangbanna are easily disturbed because they are at the very northern limit of the moist tropics. The climate of the area has recently changed, becoming cooler and drier. The forests that remain only do so because they have created their own microclimates by trapping moist air under their canopies. Young seedlings are protected from the cold by the large trees that surround them. This means that once the rain forests are destroyed they are lost for ever from the region.

Many areas of forest in Xishuangbanna have been cleared to make space for tea plantations.

63

Bamboo

Bamboo is one of the world's most remarkable plants. It is a member of the grass family – related to corn, wheat and barley – and there are over 840 different species. They are found in tropical, subtropical and warm temperate regions of the world, but the greatest variety of species grow in Southeast and southern Asia, especially in Myanmar and Thailand.

While some species form dense forests outside rain forest regions, others form extensive thickets in the rain forests themselves and can be recognized from the air. Many species of bamboo grow to more than 20 m in height. The tallest is an Indo-Malayan species, *Dendrocalamus giganteus,* which can have stems 40 m tall. Smaller kinds remain as undergrowth among the forest trees, but because their stems grow so closely together they can form impenetrable barriers.

The stems of the giant bamboo *Dendrocalamus giganteus* grow at the rate of about a metre a day.

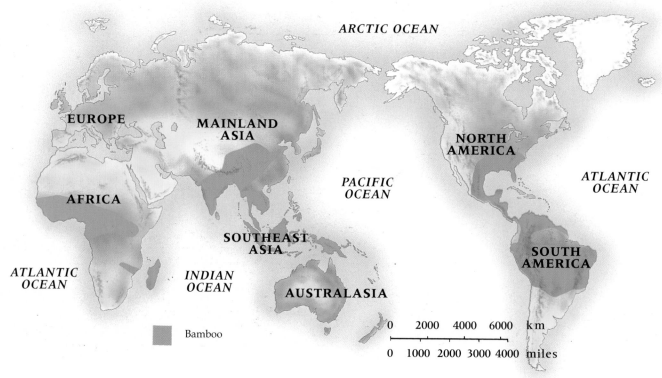

ARCTIC OCEAN

EUROPE

MAINLAND ASIA

NORTH AMERICA

PACIFIC OCEAN

ATLANTIC OCEAN

AFRICA

SOUTHEAST ASIA

SOUTH AMERICA

ATLANTIC OCEAN

INDIAN OCEAN

AUSTRALASIA

Bamboo

0   2000   4000   6000   km

0   1000 2000 3000 4000 miles

THE USES OF BAMBOO

Bamboo is used by more than half of all the people in the world, every day. Over one thousand different products have been made from bamboo stems and leaves. The stronger stems are widely used for building houses (in Myanmar and Bangladesh over half the houses are made almost entirely from bamboo), and also for scaffolding. Canes are also used for furniture and musical instruments or split and woven into baskets. Fibres are used to make rope or twine. The shoots of many kinds of bamboo are eaten and leaves are used for thatch. Bamboo is a very important source of paper in Thailand, China and Bangladesh.

Bamboos are famous for the speed at which they grow. The pointed shoots of the giant bamboos and some others can grow 1 m a day. Some species can reach their full height in only 6-8 weeks. Bamboo stems have a unique natural structure. Joints occur at regular intervals along the length of their hollow stems. The resulting lightness, flexibility and strength of the stems has made bamboo one of the most adaptable materials in the world.

Above **Bamboo stems stacked up in a bamboo factory in Leshan, China.**

Scaffolding made from whole bamboo stems is commonly used for major building projects in China and other parts of Asia.

The Sloth Bear

The sloth bear has a grey muzzle, a shaggy coat – usually black and often mixed with brown and grey – and a horseshoe-shaped marking of cream to chestnut coloured fur on its chest. It lives in India, Sri Lanka, Bangladesh, Nepal and Bhutan, in lowland dry deciduous forest as well as tropical rain forest.

Though awkward and shambling on the ground, the sloth bear, which is mainly active at night, is a good climber and can hang upside down by its claws from branches. Although it will also eat grass, flowers, fruit and crop plants, honey, bees, ants and other insects, it is uniquely adapted to eating vast quantities of termites. Using its strong curved claws to make holes in termite mounds, the bear – whose two top front teeth are missing – can form its lips into a tube and then suck out the termites like a vacuum cleaner. The noise made by the bear in this way can be heard over 200 m away, and this has helped to make it easy prey for hunters.

No one knows how many sloth bears are left in the wild, but unless conservation rules are strictly enforced this unusual bear is in danger of extinction.

Above **A sloth bear in captivity. A worldwide campaign to help stop cruelty to bears (called Libearty) has recently been set up in London.**

Bear and other animal parts on sale in China. They will be used in traditional Chinese medicine.

TIBET
(CHINA)

NEPAL

BHUTAN

PAKISTAN

Delhi

River Ganges

Ahmadabad

Calcutta

INDIA

BURMA

Bombay

Hyderabad

BANGLADESH

ARABIAN
SEA

Madras

BAY OF
BENGAL

Bangalore

Colombo

SRI LANKA

Sloth bears

| 0 | 500 | 1000 | 1500 | k m |

| 0 | 200 | 400 | 600 | 800 | miles |

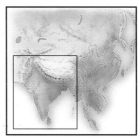

BEARS FOR EASTERN MEDICINE

Sloth bears are being hunted because different parts of their bodies fetch high prices as traditional medicines. There is an enormous trade in sloth bear gall bladders, mostly supplied by India to Japan for the supposed cure of liver and stomach problems. In 1988 alone, over 17,000 bears may have been killed for this purpose. Although the sloth bear is classified as an endangered animal by the Indian government, the illegal trade continues. In Sri Lanka, bear fat is taken and used as a hair restorer. Bear cubs are sold to circuses or as pets, and farmers consider them vermin and kill them.

A sloth bear cub in Sri Lanka. Sloth bears are omnivores (they eat both plants and animals) and wander over large areas in search of different foods.

SOUTHEAST ASIA

The rain forests of this region extend across tens of thousands of islands that lie between the south-eastern tip of continental Asia and Australia. The islands form Indonesia, part of Malaysia, and the Philippines, and their forests are extremely rich in different habitats, plants and animals. The sheer variety of plants is astonishing, and the forests contain many different kinds of palm trees, orchids and climbing plants. Southeast Asia is the home of fruits such as bananas, mangos, many citrus fruits and bread fruit. Spices like nutmeg, pepper, cinnamon and cloves also come from Southeast Asia's forests. Some of the biggest trees of the region provide much of the hardwood timber now used in the world.

Some of the world's rarest animals are found in Southeast Asia, including Javan and Sumatran rhinoceroses, orang-utans, tigers and several species of deer.

There have been people living in Southeast Asia for more than 500,000 years, and millions of tribal people continue to inhabit the rain forests today. However, rapid industrialization, population growth and colonization schemes have led to the destruction of forests at an alarming rate.

Most of the rain forest on the 13,000 islands of Indonesia is threatened by widespread deforestation for logging and agriculture. Java, one of the most densely populated islands in the world, has now lost 90 per cent of its natural vegetation. However, Indonesia still has 1.1 million square kilometres of rain forest, which is almost 40 per cent of all the rain forest in Asia and nearly 10 per cent of all the rain forest on earth.

The dense rain forests on the island of Borneo are one of the most diverse ecosystems in the world.

68

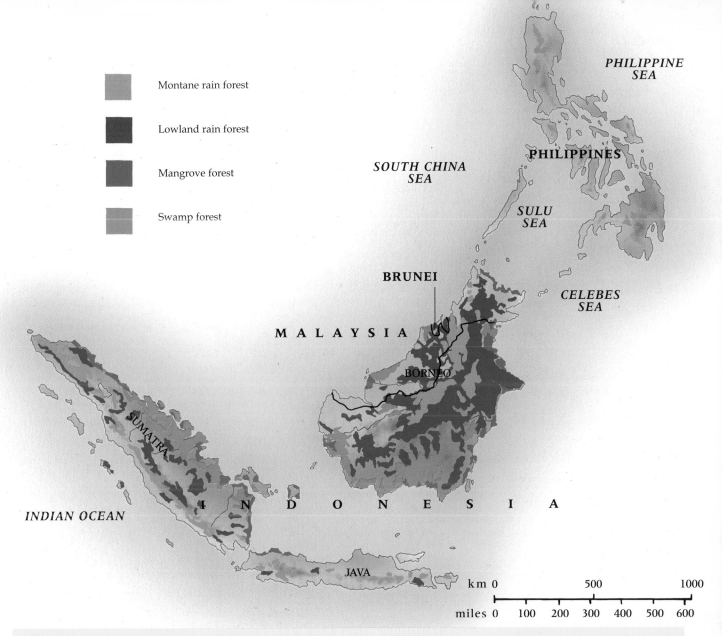

Montane rain forest

Lowland rain forest

Mangrove forest

Swamp forest

PHILIPPINE SEA

SOUTH CHINA SEA

PHILIPPINES

SULU SEA

BRUNEI

CELEBES SEA

M A L A Y S I A

BORNEO

SUMATRA

I N D O N E S I A

INDIAN OCEAN

JAVA

km 0   500   1000

miles 0   100   200   300   400   500   600

THE WORLD'S BIGGEST FLOWER

One of the most spectacular of Southeast Asia's plants is the giant *Rafflesia arnoldii*. It is a parasitic plant that feeds on the roots of certain climbing vines. The only part of the plant that can be seen above ground is its enormous flower, which can measure over a metre across. This is the largest flower in the world. It smells of rotting meat, to attract the flies which pollinate it.

In order to help attract flies, the colours of the giant *rafflesia* flower imitate those of rotting meat.

69

The Penan

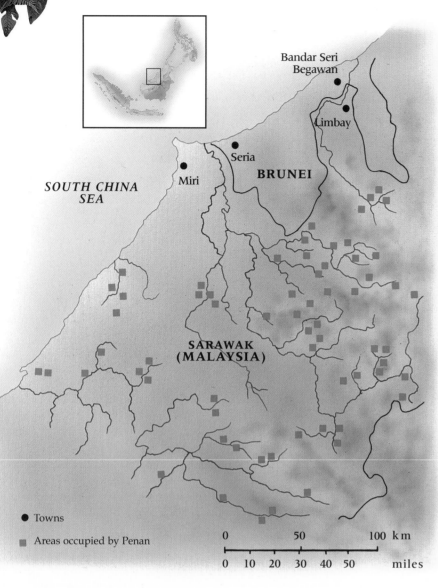

SOUTH CHINA SEA

Bandar Seri Begawan

Limbay

Seria

Miri

BRUNEI

SARAWAK
(MALAYSIA)

● Towns

■ Areas occupied by Penan

0   50   100 k m

0 10 20 30 40 50   miles

The Penan are one of many tribal peoples, known together as the Dyaks, who live in the rain forests of Sarawak, on the island of Borneo. The Dyaks have lived in the rain forests for thousands of years. Most of them are settled farmers who grow crops such as rice and live in longhouses. The Penan, though, are traditionally nomadic hunter-gatherers, who do not practise agriculture.

Families live in simple thatched shelters – *sulaps* – and build a new one on a new site every few weeks. They gather a wide range of foods from the forest, including wild sago, which forms the basis of their diet, and hunt animals, especially wild pigs, for meat. Penan men are very skilful hunters and can kill a gibbon in the tree tops from 50 m away using a blowpipe and poison darts.

Below A Penan man with a wild boar he has killed in the forest.

The Penan believe in the power of forest spirits. They do not like to cut down trees to build longhouses, or even to make room for crops, out of respect for the spirits. However, their traditional lifestyle has recently been drastically upset. Since 1987 logging companies have been invading the forest of the Penan and other Dyak peoples in a rush to cut down as much timber as possible. This has caused enormous destruction to the forest and its wildlife. Many Penan have now been forced to settle in permanent houses, and to give up their ancient way of life.

Left A Penan tribesman preparing wild boar meat for cooking. Behind him is the traditional *sulap*, a simple shelter.

LOGS OR PEOPLE?

The Dyak's forest in Sarawak is being destroyed faster than any other rain forest in the world. Over one-third has disappeared already, and plans exist to log most of the rest. Because neither the loggers nor the Malaysian government would listen to them, the Penan set up road-blocks to try to protect their forest. But the government has made interference with logging a criminal offence and many Penan have been sent to prison or fined.

'We put up the blockades because we don't want any further destruction [done] to our land.'

Penan man from Long Latik.

Below Penan men on a road made by loggers.

Birdwing Butterflies

The twelve species of birdwing butterfly are the biggest and among the most spectacular butterflies in the world. The name birdwing refers to the shape of the butterfly's forewings, which are larger and more slender than the hind wings. This makes them look like birds as they fly through the upper layers of the rain forest.

Female butterflies are generally larger, but the males are more colourful. Their velvety wings are often streaked with gleaming gold, amber or emerald. Adult birdwings live solitary lives and are very active during the day, collecting nectar from the flowers of forest trees.

One of the most impressive birdwings is Rajah Brooke's, which has a wingspan of up to 19 cm and is found on the islands of Borneo and Sumatra and in mainland Malaysia. The largest birdwing is Queen Alexandra's – females have a wingspan of over 28 cm. This butterfly is now found only in a small area in the Northern Province of Papua New Guinea.

The birdwings' spectacular size and colouration have made them the target of butterfly collectors, and the larger birdwings were once killed with bows and arrows to supply the trade. While all birdwings are now threatened by the relentless destruction of their forest home, in some areas butterfly farming is helping to prevent them from being wiped out completely.

POISON WARNING

The spectacular colours of birdwing butterflies act as a warning to predators that they are poisonous. They do not produce their own poisons but accumulate them as caterpillars by feeding on poisonous vegetation, especially certain forest vines, with no harm to themselves.

A birdwing butterfly from Indonesia. With its stunning colours, it is easy to see why collectors wanted them.

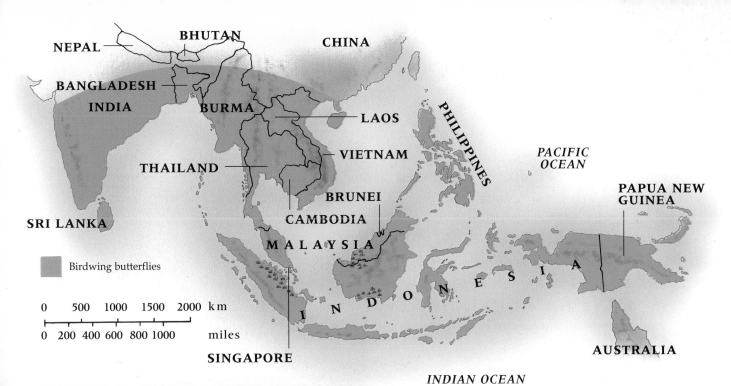

NEPAL — BHUTAN — CHINA
BANGLADESH
INDIA — BURMA
LAOS
THAILAND — VIETNAM
SRI LANKA
BRUNEI
CAMBODIA
MALAYSIA
PHILIPPINES
PACIFIC OCEAN
PAPUA NEW GUINEA
INDONESIA
SINGAPORE
AUSTRALIA

Birdwing butterflies

0   500 1000 1500 2000 km
0 200 400 600 800 1000   miles

INDIAN OCEAN

Left These Rajah Brooke's birdwing butterflies were bred on a butterfly farm. They are being mounted for sale.

Below The leaves of *Aristolochia* vines are a major food of birdwing caterpillars.

73

Rattans

Rattans are thorny climbing palms. They have long, rope-like stems and grow high up into the forest canopy. Rattans use backward-curving spines attached to long, thin tendrils at the ends of their leaf stems to climb other trees. There are hundreds of different kinds of rattan, and the biggest can grow to a length of about 200 m, though 75 m is an average length. The greatest concentrations are in mainland Malaysia and on Borneo.

The people of South and Southeast Asia have been using rattans for a variety of purposes for thousands of years. Today, they are the most important product of Southeast Asia's tropical forests after timber, and are worth hundreds of millions of pounds a year in exports. About 150,000 tonnes of rattans are harvested each year, almost entirely from the wild. About half a million people make their living by harvesting and processing the stems. Most rattans are made into furniture, for export all over the world, while other uses include rope and baskets. The Philippines and Indonesia are both major exporters of rattan products.

Above Spines and twisting tendrils enable rattans to climb high into the forest canopy.

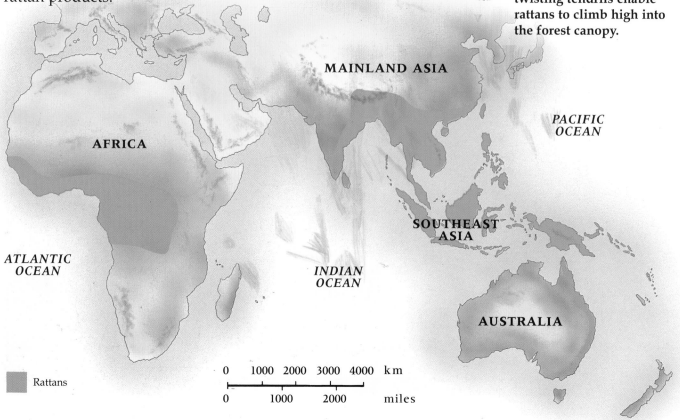

MAINLAND ASIA

PACIFIC OCEAN

AFRICA

SOUTHEAST ASIA

ATLANTIC OCEAN

INDIAN OCEAN

AUSTRALIA

■ Rattans

| 0 | 1000 | 2000 | 3000 | 4000 | km |
| 0 | | 1000 | | 2000 | miles |

Although some plantations have now been set up, many species of rattan are threatened in the wild because of the rate at which they are being harvested. The forests on which they depend for survival are also quickly disappearing through logging and settlement.

USES OF RATTAN

After they have been pulled out of the trees that support them, rattan stems are cut into lengths of 3–5 m and then dried for about a month. After grading, they are washed, and then scoured with sand before bleaching. While the thicker canes are often used for furniture frames, others may be split into fine strands for chair backs, seating, basketry and decorative screens. In the Philippines rattans are also made into fish traps, sleeping mats, hammocks, hats, walking sticks and toothbrushes, and the young shoots are eaten as a vegetable.

Above A sofa panel being woven from rattan canes in Manila, Philippines.

Below Rattan furniture being driven to market in Thailand.

The Orang-Utan

The orang-utan is the only great ape in Asia. There are two different kinds: one lives only on the island of Borneo and the other only on Sumatra. The name orang-utan means 'man of the forest' in the Malay language.

Orang-utans are the largest tree-living mammals in the world and can weigh up to 90 kg. They are well adapted for life in the trees. Their arms are extremely long and powerful: when standing up their arms reach down to their ankles, and they measure up to 2.25 m from finger tip to finger tip when spread out.

Orang-utans spend most of their lives in the trees and are rarely seen on the ground. They move by climbing and walking through the larger trees, and by swinging from branch to branch. They live in many different types of tropical rain forest, from swamp and lowland forests at sea level to montane forests at up to 1,800 m.

Orang-utans eat fruit, nuts, leaves, bark, eggs and insects. They are particularly fond of wild figs and durian fruit. Durians are large, spine-covered fruits which have a delicious taste but a strong, unpleasant smell.

The orang-utan's feet are as useful as its hands. Here hanging upside down, the orang-utan drinks from a rain-forest stream.

No one knows exactly how many orang-utans are left in the wild, but the destruction of their forest home and the capture of babies for the pet trade is continuing to reduce their numbers.

MOTHERS AND BABIES

Male and female orang-utans live separate lives but can breed at any time because food is plentiful all year round. Females usually give birth to a single baby every three to six years. They spend a long time bringing up each infant, and do not mate again until the young are at least three years old. Because of this females may only have two or three babies during their lifetime.

Above New-born orang-utans are totally dependent on their mothers for the first 18 months of their lives.

The Sumatran Rhino

The Sumatran rhino is the smallest of the five species of rhinoceros that live in Africa and Asia. Its body is about 2.6 m long and 1.35 m tall. Although it is the smallest rhino species, males can weigh up to 1 tonne.

Sumatran rhinos tend to be solitary animals, with the exception of mothers nursing their young. Despite their clumsy appearance, they are agile and are equally at home in dense forests or on steep mountain sides. Their foot prints have been found at heights of 2,000 m.

Sumatran rhinos are being bred in captivity to try to increase their numbers.

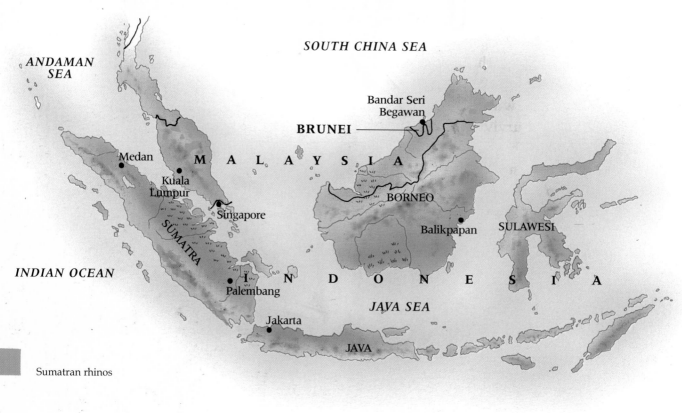

Sumatran rhinos

| 0 | 500 | 1000 | k m |

| 0 | 100 | 200 | 300 | 400 | 500 | 600 | miles |

Above **Wild mangoes make a delicious addition to the diet of Sumatran rhinos.**

Sumatran rhinos usually feed twice a day – in the early morning and in the evening. Their main food is the branches of young bushes and trees, but they also eat fruit such as wild figs and mangoes. Each rhino spends the hottest part of the day and the middle of the night wallowing in its own mud hollow. Covering their skin in thick mud protects the rhinos from biting insects.

These shy animals prefer to live in forests that are undisturbed by people. Until relatively recently they were found throughout Southeast Asia, but today the main populations are restricted to the rain forests of Sumatra and mainland Malaysia. Their population has dropped to about 500 individuals, and like their even rarer relative, the Javan rhino, they are in danger of becoming extinct.

THE MOST ANCIENT RHINO

Fossil records show that rhinos have existed for around 50 million years and that there may have been as many as 300 different species in the past. The Sumatran rhino is the most ancient rhino species left today and is the only one with hairy skin. It is the last surviving member of one of the prehistoric rhino families and differs little from rhinos that lived 40 million years ago.

The rare Sumatran rhino is among the most endangered of all animals in the world.

AUSTRALASIA

Over 135 million years ago Australia, New Zealand, New Guinea and neighbouring islands were joined together, forming part of the great southern landmass of Gondwanaland. At that time dense tropical rain forest covered the moist coastal area. As Gondwanaland broke up and the islands drifted apart, many distinct new forms of life developed that became unique to each island. However, millions of years later there are still strong similarities among their animals and plants.

TROPICAL RAIN FORESTS

The largest area of tropical rain forest remaining in the region is on the island of New Guinea, and covers about 700,000 square kilometres. It is extremely rich in plants, with over 20,000 species. Some types of tree have enormous canopies, stretching for 50 m or more. The smaller trees and plants that grow in the shade of the forest giants include tree ferns, palms, gingers and orchids. Much of the landscape is mountainous and at around 3,000 m the forests are dominated by southern beech. Other trees include the giant gum – the world's tallest flowering plant – which can grow up to 100 m tall.

New Guinea is famous for its extraordinary bird and animal life, including birds of paradise, cassowaries and cockatoos, as well as marsupials such as echidnas, tree kangaroos, and quolls.

Unlike New Guinea, there are only small patches of tropical rain forest in Australia. These are found in three main areas along the north-east coastal region of the State of Queensland, covering about 10,500 square kilometres in total. Although Australia's rain forests are not as rich in species as those of New Guinea, about eight out of every ten of its 2,500 flowering plants are found nowhere else in the world.

TEMPERATE RAIN FORESTS

Large areas of coastal temperate rain forest are found only in Tasmania and New Zealand, although there are small areas in mainland Australia. Tasmania still has about 85 per cent of its original forest, covering up to 760,000 ha. Logging has been banned since 1982, but only 45 per cent of the forest is protected in reserves and national parks.

The extensive temperate rain forests of New Zealand cover about 5,360,000 ha, which is around 15 per cent of the original lowland forest. Most occurs on the west coast of South Island, although North Island has some small areas of subtropical forest.

Banksia plants, also known as Australian honeysuckles, make a colourful addition to the rain forest foliage.

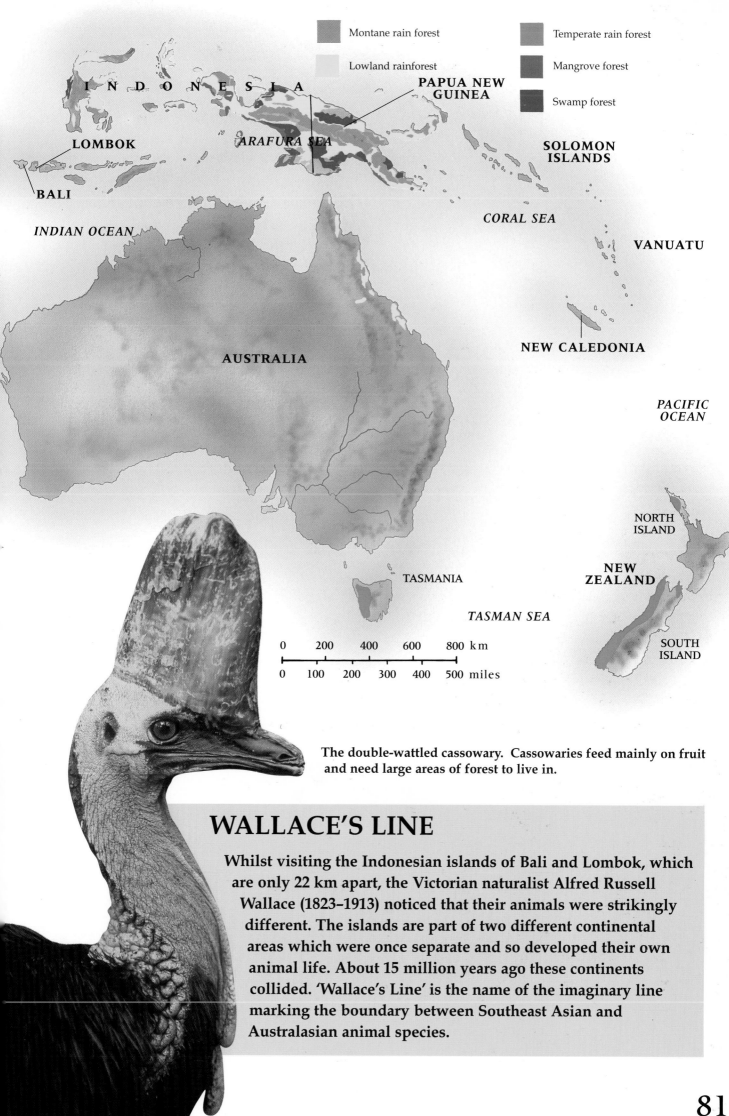

Montane rain forest

Lowland rainforest

Temperate rain forest

Mangrove forest

Swamp forest

I N D O N E S I A

PAPUA NEW GUINEA

LOMBOK

ARAFURA SEA

SOLOMON ISLANDS

BALI

INDIAN OCEAN

CORAL SEA

VANUATU

AUSTRALIA

NEW CALEDONIA

PACIFIC OCEAN

NORTH ISLAND

NEW ZEALAND

TASMANIA

TASMAN SEA

SOUTH ISLAND

0	200	400	600	800	km
0	100	200	300	400	500	miles

The double-wattled cassowary. Cassowaries feed mainly on fruit and need large areas of forest to live in.

WALLACE'S LINE

Whilst visiting the Indonesian islands of Bali and Lombok, which are only 22 km apart, the Victorian naturalist Alfred Russell Wallace (1823–1913) noticed that their animals were strikingly different. The islands are part of two different continental areas which were once separate and so developed their own animal life. About 15 million years ago these continents collided. 'Wallace's Line' is the name of the imaginary line marking the boundary between Southeast Asian and Australasian animal species.

The Huli

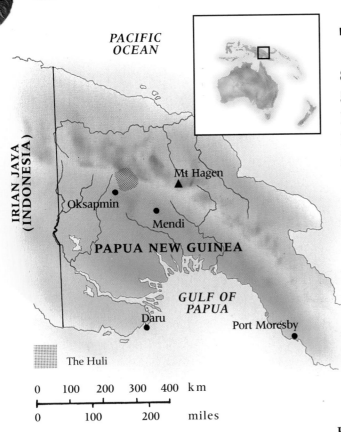

PACIFIC OCEAN

IRIAN JAYA (INDONESIA)

Oksapmin

Mt Hagen

Mendi

PAPUA NEW GUINEA

GULF OF PAPUA

Daru

Port Moresby

The Huli

| 0 | 100 | 200 | 300 | 400 | km |

| 0 | 100 | 200 | miles |

The Huli are one of the largest indigenous groups in Papua New Guinea. About 80,000 Huli people live in a territory of about 5,200 square kilometres in Southern Highlands Province. This mountainous landscape is very varied; as well as dense rain forest there are swamps, grassy plains, and steep cliffs and gorges.

The Huli grow a number of crops to provide food for themselves. The main one is the sweet potato, though they also grow taro, sugar cane, bananas, pumpkins, corn and green leaf vegetables. The sweet potatoes are generally roasted over embers, or steamed with other vegetables in a special pit in the ground.

Huli men take face and body decoration very seriously.

The Huli often grow useful plants immediately outside their houses, as well as in forest clearings.

Huli men and women lead largely separate lives. The men live together in communal houses, while women have their own individual huts. The women's huts are often built close to their gardens, which they tend carefully by weeding and adding compost. Girls start helping to look after their brothers and sisters at a young age, and must also look after the family's pigs.

Huli men dig up their own sweet potatoes, cook their own food and generally look after themselves. Like other traditional tribespeople of New Guinea, the men take great pride in their appearance: they decorate their faces and bodies with coloured clays, charcoal and – more recently – bright artificial paints.

HULI WIGS

Huli men's wigs are usually made from human hair which is matted into shape using sharp bamboo sticks. They are mostly triangular or semi-circular, curving downward over the head. Often coloured with powdered ochre pigment, many wigs are also decorated with yellow everlasting daisies and bird of paradise feathers.

Inside a men's house Huli men socialize and prepare their own food, away from the women.

Birds of Paradise

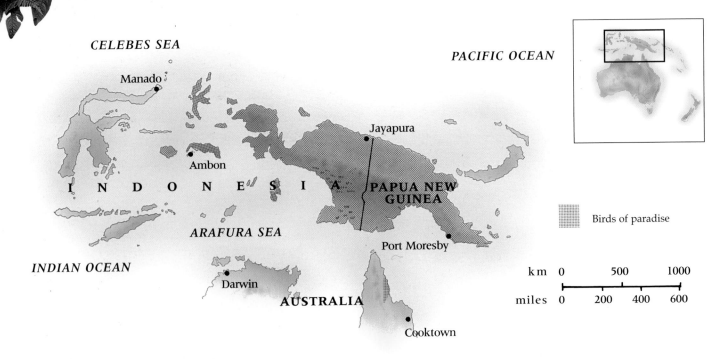

CELEBES SEA

PACIFIC OCEAN

Manado

Jayapura

Ambon

I N D O N E S I A   PAPUA NEW GUINEA

ARAFURA SEA

Port Moresby

INDIAN OCEAN

Darwin

AUSTRALIA

Cooktown

Birds of paradise

km   0   500   1000

miles 0   200   400   600

Birds of paradise were given their name when the Spanish royal court was first shown some of their feathers during the sixteenth century. The feathers were so beautiful it was decided that they must have come from paradise.

There are 43 species of birds of paradise: 37 are found in the dense rain forests of New Guinea, while the rest are spread across northern Australia, the Moluccas and the Aru Islands.

The females tend to be dull, often brownish in colour, but the males have magnificent multicoloured feathers which gleam in the light. They are also adorned with all kinds of crests, fans, plumes and tail streamers. Among the most beautiful are the blue bird of paradise and the raggiana bird of paradise.

The indigenous peoples of New Guinea have always used bird of paradise feathers for their elaborate headdresses, but this has had relatively little effect on the birds' numbers.

The beautiful male raggiana bird of paradise often displays in trees at the edges of villages in New Guinea.

The male red bird of paradise performs his courtship display upside down.

COURTSHIP DISPLAYS

Male birds of paradise perform a great variety of elaborate displays to attract females. Some compete at communal display grounds, or leks, and give dazzling performances of colour and sound. Lesser birds of paradise gather in tall tree-tops and shriek a dawn chorus, displaying their golden tail feathers over their backs. Blue birds of paradise perform dramatic upside-down displays, fanning out breast and wing feathers so that they catch the light and hypnotize the females. Magnificent birds of paradise often remove leaves just above their display grounds, so that a spotlight of sunshine illuminates their dance.

It was only when the birds began to be systematically hunted by others, to supply European hat-makers, that their populations were seriously reduced. In the late nineteenth century, feathers from about 50,000 birds were being exported every year. Trade was finally banned in the 1920s. Today it is loss of habitat through logging and mining that is the major threat to many species.

This New Guinea man is wearing a magnificent head-dress decorated with feathers from several different kinds of bird of paradise.

Tree Kangaroos

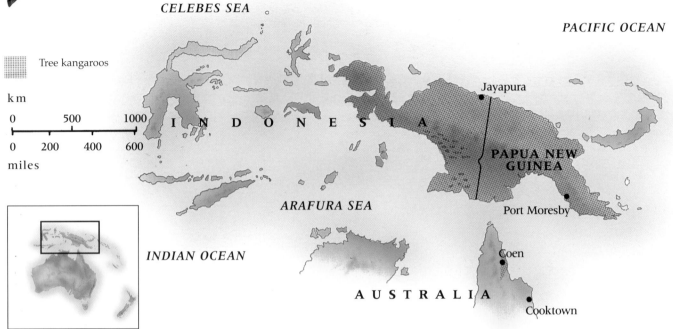

CELEBES SEA

PACIFIC OCEAN

Tree kangaroos

km

| 0 | 500 | 1000 |

| 0 | 200 | 400 | 600 |

miles

INDONESIA

Jayapura

PAPUA NEW
GUINEA

ARAFURA SEA

Port Moresby

INDIAN OCEAN

Coen

AUSTRALIA

Cooktown

Tree kangaroos look quite different from their ground-living cousins, but like all marsupials they carry their young in a pouch. There are eight different species: two living in north-east Australia and the others in New Guinea.

Tree kangaroos are found mostly in mountainous areas at heights of up to 3,000 m or more. They vary in size from about 50–80 cm in length, with tails 40–90 cm long.

A Goodfellows tree kangaroo enjoying a meal of wild figs.

Goodfellows tree kangaroo is one of the most brightly coloured of all marsupials. This female has a baby in her pouch.

Tree kangaroos are perfectly adapted to life in the tree canopy. Unlike ground-living kangaroos, their front legs are almost as long as their back legs and they walk rather than hop, using their long tails for balancing. They are extremely agile and can move rapidly from tree to tree, leaping up to 9 m between branches. They are generally solitary animals and spend most of the day resting or asleep on high branches. They are most active at night, when they feed on the forest's plentiful supply of leaves and fruit. Tree kangaroos also regularly visit the ground and can jump down from a height of 18 m or more.

Tree kangaroos are now generally threatened in New Guinea, because of the increasing use of guns for hunting.

THE 'NEW' TREE KANGAROO

In 1994 biologists were able to confirm that an eighth species of tree kangaroo existed. Its scientific name is *Dendrolagus mbaiso*. It lives in south-eastern Irian Jaya in an extremely rugged habitat – a stunted, mossy forest clinging to steep mountainsides at around 4,000 m. The region is often bitterly cold and continuously shrouded in mist.

Although unknown to Westerners, it was already well known to the Moni people of the Maokop mountains, who regard it as an ancestor and do not hunt it. They believe that its behaviour of throwing its arms up in the air and whistling when frightened shows that it is related to humans. Their name for it is *dingiso*, which means 'the forbidden animal'.

A Dani tribesman holds the tree kangaroo that was only recently discovered by scientists.

The Kauri Pine

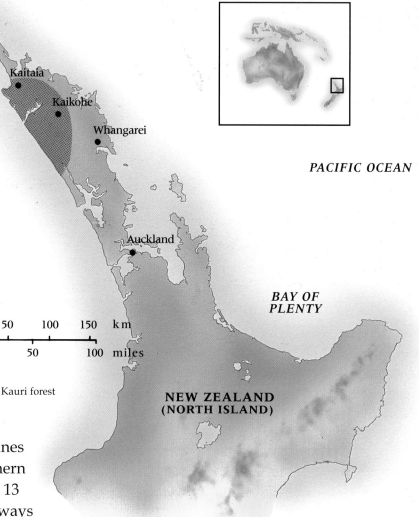

Kauri pines are native to the North Island of New Zealand. They are remarkable trees because of the great age and size they reach. They live for about 2,000 years and can grow up to 55 m tall, with an enormous girth. Their trunks are extremely straight and even, and barely taper from ground level to the first branch. Mature kauri pines have huge branches which are home to other groups of plants, especially epiphytes. The trees are also famous for the resin they produce, known as kauri gum or copal.

Until the arrival of Europeans in New Zealand, kauri pines formed extensive forests in the northern part of North Island, covering about 13 million ha. These giant trees have always been sacred to the Maori people – who know the largest by individual names – and they were never cut down. However, their very tough, straight timber made them highly sought-after by *pakeha* (non-Maoris) for building ships and houses. Kauri trees were thoughtlessly cut down for many years and it was not until 1974 that the destruction was stopped. Today, only about 400,000 ha still exist, the largest area being in the Waipuoa forest.

Although kauris are protected in the wild today, they are often too far from one another to reproduce naturally. To try and increase their numbers, some trees are being hand-pollinated by biologists who are lowered close to the canopy from a hovering helicopter.

Right **This immense kauri tree, in the Waipuoa forest, is called *Tane Mahuta* which means 'God of the forest' in Maori. It is 51 m tall.**

DINOSAUR FOOD

The kauri pine is a member of an ancient family of trees that dominated the forests of the southern hemisphere over 230 million years ago. They are thought to have been an important food for some of the dinosaurs that roamed the planet and their fossils have been found from Antarctica to Scotland.

Glossary

BUTTRESS ROOTS Roots which grow from the trunk of a tree above the ground, helping to support it.

CONIFER An evergreen tree which usually has cones.

CHICLERO A person who collects the sap from chicle trees.

CAMOUFLAGE Colours or shapes which blend in with the surroundings.

COLONIZATION People moving into an area in order to settle there.

CONSERVATIONIST A person who believes that nature should be protected.

CANOPY The uppermost layer of branches formed by a tree or trees.

DECIDUOUS FOREST A forest containing trees that shed their leaves each year.

DEFORESTATION The removal of trees from an area.

ECOSYSTEM A community of different species and the environment they live in.

FLOODED FOREST An area of forest which is flooded permanently or at certain times of the year.

HABITAT The natural home of a particular plant or animal.

INDIGENOUS Belonging originally or naturally to a particular place.

LONGHOUSE A large, traditional house shared by many families.

LATEX A milky sap that is produced by various plants and trees.

MONSOON FOREST Tropical forest found in Asia, where there are distinct dry and rainy seasons and in which trees lose their leaves each year.

MICROCLIMATE The climate of a small, local area.

MANGROVE FOREST Evergreen forest found along some tropical coastlines. The trees have special roots that stick up from the mud and can take in oxygen.

MONTANE FOREST Forest which occurs above 900 metres above sea level.

NOCTURNAL Active at night.

NOMADIC Describes people who do not have any one home location but move regularly.

OCEANIC CLIMATE A climate strongly influenced by an ocean.

OCHRE A type of clay which varies in colour from light yellow to brown or red.

PLUMAGE A bird's feathers.

PLANTATIONS Areas in which single crops are planted, often in rows.

PARASITE A plant or animal benefitting by living on another one.

PREDATOR An animal which hunts another one.

PREHENSILE Being able to coil up the tail and use it as a fifth limb.

REGURGITATE To bring swallowed food up into the mouth again.

RICE PADDY A field where rice is grown.

SAGO A kind of starchy food made from the pith of the sago palm.

SAPLING A young tree.

SUBTROPICS Areas of the world bordering the tropics.

TEMPERATE A mild or moderate climate.

TROPICS The area with high temperatures and rainfall between the tropics of Cancer and Capricorn, 23° north and south of the Equator.

VENOM A poisonous liquid produced by some snakes, scorpions and spiders.

Further Information

USEFUL ADDRESSES

Friends of the Earth

26–28 Underwood Street

London N1 7JQ

Tel: 0171 490 1555

website: www.foe.co.uk

Reforest the Earth

48 Bethel Street

Norwich

Norfolk NR2 1NR

Tel: 01603 631007

Survival International

11–15 Emerald Street

London WC1N 3QL

Tel: 0207 242 1441

website: www.survival.org.uk

The Living Earth Foundation

Warwick House

106 Harrow Road

London W2 1XD

Tel: 0207 258 1823

WWF-UK

Panda House

Weyside Park

Catteshall Lane

Godalming

Surrey GU7 1XR

Tel: 01483 426444

website: www.wwf-uk.org

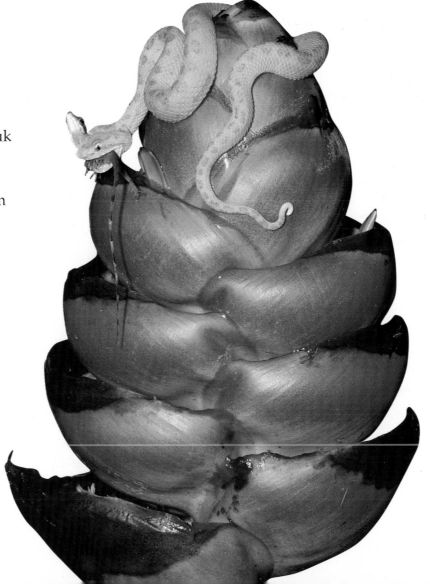

BOOKS TO READ

Antonio's Rainforest by Anna Lewington (Wayland, 1992)

Baka: People of the Rainforest by Lisa Silcock (Channel 4 Television, 1988). A book that accompanies Phil Agland's film of the same name (see opposite).

Brazil: Advanced Case Studies (Hodder & Stoughton, 1998)

Discovering the Amazon by the editors of Reader's Digest books (Reader's Digest, 1994)

Jungle by Theresa Greenaway (Dorling Kindersley, 1994)

Jungles & Rainforests by Steve Parker (Belitha Press, 1996)

The Last Rain Forests ed. Mark Collins (Mitchell Beazley, 1990)

Life in the Rainforest (Two-Can Publishing, 1994)

People of the Rainforest by Edward Parker & Anna Lewington (Wayland, 1998)

Sacha Mama: Mother Jungle A case study of a sustainable development scheme in the Amazonian forest. (Actionaid, 1996)

Stories from the Amazon by Saviour Pirotta (Wayland, 1999)

Up a Rainforest Tree by Carole Telford and Rod Theodorou (Heinemann, 1998)

OTHER RESOURCES

Rainforests for Tomorrow A 16 page A4 colour booklet looking at the location, structure and uses of the world's rainforests. (Worldaware, 1999)

The Emerald's Crown Musical on audio-cassette with voice and piano score.

(WWF-UK, 1991)

Exploring Brazil Mapcards A pack of 15 laminated map cards. (Hodder & Stoughton)

In Search of Eldorado Background information and activities which examine some of the major social and economic issues in Brazil today. (Trocaire, 1996)

Land for the Landless Board game which explores population migration in Brazil. (Actionaid)

MULTI-MEDIA PACKS

The Decade of Destruction Teacher's book and video (WWF-UK, 1986/Central Independent Television, 1991)

Interfact: Rainforests Book and CD-Rom (Two-Can, 1998)

FILMS AND VIDEOS

EDUCATIONAL

The Decade of Destruction by Adrian Cowell (Central Independent Television, 1991)

The Flooded Forest by Michael Goulding (BBC)

Vietnam: After the Fire by Edward Milner (Channel 4/Acacia Productions, 1988)

Greening Thailand by Edward Milner (Channel 4/Acacia Productions, 1990)

Baka: People of the Rain Forest by Phil Agland (DJA River Films for Channel 4, 1987)

Nomads of the Wind by (BBC, 1995)

FEATURE FILMS

The Emerald Forest (Embassy Pictures, 1985)

The Mission (Goldcrest Films, 1985)

Gorillas in the Mist (Warner Bros, 1988)

Medicine Man (Cinergi, 1992)

Index

Picture Acknowledgements

Bruce Coleman Ltd 4tl/M P L Fogden, 27b/Luiz Claudio Marigo, 56/Nigel Blake, 86/C B and D W Frith; B V Devaraj 60, 61t; NHPA 24/Kevin Schafer, 42b/Eric Soder, 49b/Daniel Heuclin; Oxford Scientific Films 10/Richard Alan Wood/Animals Animals, 12t/Stan Osolinski, 14/Ronald Tims, 15/Dr F Koster/Survival Anglia, 18t, 18b/Deni Bown, 19 Daniel J Cox, 20/Lon E Lauber, 21b/Richard Alan Wood/Animals Animals, 25l/Michael Fogden, 26/Chris Sharp, 27t/Chris Sharp, 28/Michael Fogden, 29t/Frank Schneidermeyer, 29b/Michael Fogden, 31t/David Cayless, 37/Nick Gordon/Survival Anglia, 37b/Michael Goulding, 39t/Nick Gordon/Survival Anglia, 40/Nick Gordon/Survival Anglia, 41t/Nick Gordon/Survival Anglia, 41b/John Mitchell/Photo Researchers, 43t/M Wendler/Okapia, 46t/Nick Gordon/Survival Anglia, 50t/David Haring, 50b/Konrad Wothe, 51/David Haring, 63t/Tony Tilford, 64/Deni Bown, 66t/Zig Leszczynski/Animals Animals, 67/Alan and Sandy Carey, 72/E R Degginger/Photo Researchers, 73t/Harold Taylor, 73b/Mantis Wildlife Films, 74/Deni Bown, 75t/C Prescott-Allen/Earth Scenes, 76/Konrad Wothe, 83t/Michael Pitts, 83b/Michael Pitts, 84/Michael McCoy/Photo Researchers, 85t/Tom McHugh/Photo Researchers, 87t/Tom McHugh/Photo Researchers; Edward Parker 36, 38-9, 45, 44-5, 52t, 53; Sealaska Corporation 11b/Mark Kelley, 16, 17t, 17b/Mark Kelley; South American Pictures 34/Marion Morrison, 35b/Tony Morrison; Still Pictures 1/Margaret Wilson, 9t/Mark Edwards, 9b/Roland Seitre, 12b/Daniel Dancer, 32t/Michael Gunther, 32b/Mark Edwards, 42-3/Y J Rey-Millet, 46-7/André Maslennikov, 48/Margaret Wilson, 49t/Margaret Wilson, 52b/Mark Edward, 54t/Mark Carwardine, 54b/T Geer, 55/Michael Gunther, 57l/Dominique Halleux, 57r/Edward Parker, 58-9/M Harvey, 68/Fred Hoogervorst, 69b/Roland Seitre, 70/Nigel Dickinson, 71t/Nigel Dickinson, 71b/Nigel Dickinson, 75b/Mark Edwards, 77t/J Alcalay and B Marcon, 77b/Michael Gunther, 78/Louise Murray, 79b/Roland Seitre, 80/Klein and Hubert, 81/Klein and Hubert; Tony Stone Images 21t/Art Wolfe, 22/Nigel Atherton, 23b/Ed Rooney, 82/Glen Allison; Trip 8/Eric Smith, 11t/W Jacobs, 23t/R Belbin, 61b/F Good, 65t/F Good, 79t, 85b/Eric Smith, 89/W Jacobs; Werner Forman Archive 25r/Liverpool Museum, Liverpool; David Woodfall 65b/Nigel Hicks; World Parrot Trust 30, 31b; WWF 35t/Hartmut Jungius, 62/Paul Sochacewski, 63b/Soh Koon Chng, 66b/Terry Domico, 87b/Gerald S Cubitt.